Judaism for AS students

by Lavinia Cohn-Sherbok and Wendy Dossett

Series Editor: Roger J Owen

Acknowledgements
The authors would like to thank: *Patch Cockburn; Jackie Factor;* and especially members of the *Swansea Hebrew Congregation*, whose contributions to the book were invaluable.

Credits

Cover: DH98593 Passover Meal, 1997 (oil on canvas) by Dora Holzhandler (contemporary artist), Private Collection/Bridgeman Art Library.
Collection Jewish Historical Museum Amsterdam: p. 4. Reprinted by permission of Oxford University Press: p. 7(t). Swansea Hebrew Congregation: p. 8, 9, 16, 19, 42(b), 47, 76(t), 80, 83. World Religions/COPIX: p. 10, 42(t), 48, 81, 90.
The Bodleian Library, University of Oxford: p. 11 (Ms. Kennicott 1, f 305r).
The Jerusalem Publishing House Ltd., Jerusalem: p. 13. Photo Wiener Library, London: p. 17.
Rex Features Limited: p. 21. Library of the Hungarian Academy of Sciences: p. 23 (Kaufmann Ms A.50). Atlas of Jewish History, Dan Cohn-Sherbok, Routledge, 1994 (p. 65): p. 29. Werner Braun, Jerusalem: p. 34. Jewish Chronicle: p. 41, 46, 57(t), 60, 64, 66, 78.
Liba Taylor/Hutchison Picture Library: p. 57(b), 65(t), 79, 88. Tegwyn Roberts: p. 44.
Kathie Dossett: p. 51, Wendy Dossett: 91. Brenda Prince/Format Photographers: p. 56.
The Jewish Catalog, Richard Siegal, Michael Strassfeld and Sharon Strassfeld, The Jewish Publication Society of America, Philadelphia: p. 58, 87. The Associated Press Ltd.: p. 65(b).
Miriam Reik/Format Photographers: p. 74(t), 77. The Second Jewish Catalog, S. and M. Strassfeld, 1976 (p. 40), The Jewish Publication Society of America, Philadelphia: p. 74(b).
Joshua Liss: p. 76(b).

Roger J. Owen, Series Editor
Roger J. Owen was Head of RE in a variety of schools for thirty years, as well as being a Head of Faculty, advisory teacher for primary and secondary RE, Section 23 Inspector and 'O' Level and GCSE Chief Examiner. Author of seventeen educational titles, he is currently an education consultant and WJEC Religious Studies AS and A2 Chair of Examiners.

Published by UWIC Press
UWIC, Cyncoed Road,
Cardiff CF23 6XD
cgrove@uwic.ac.uk
029 2041 6515

ISBN 1-902724-62-3

Design by *the info group*
Picture research by *Gwenda Lloyd Wallace*
Printed by *HSW Print*

Commissioned with the financial assistance of Awdurdod Cymwysterau, Cwricwlwm ac Asesu Cymru / the Qualifications, Curriculum and Assessment Authority for Wales (ACCAC).

Judaism
for AS students

by Lavinia Cohn-Sherbok
and Wendy Dossett
Series Editor: Roger J Owen

Contents

Judaism

Introduction

This book is written primarily for students studying AS level Judaism in Wales. Commissioned by ACCAC, it takes account of the Curriculum Cymreig, otherwise stated as the need for pupils to be "given opportunities, where appropriate, to develop and apply their knowledge and understanding of the cultural, economic, environmental, historical and linguistic characteristics of Wales." As such many of its references and examples have a Welsh flavour. This is an appropriate emphasis in a book which has been commissioned, written, and marketed in a Welsh context. It does not mean the book cannot be used in England or elsewhere.

The book assumes no prior knowledge of Judaism, and presents the religion in such a way as to meet the requirements of the WJEC AS specification. However, under no circumstances should this book be used as the sole textbook for the Judaism course, since advanced study requires the skills of wide reading, and the analysis of a range of scholarly views of different issues.

The book is designed to be used in tandem with the teachers' book, which provides more detailed background information on some of the topics covered, and assistance with the tasks that appear in the text.

AS level candidates are expected to demonstrate not only knowledge and understanding, but also certain skills, such as the ability to sustain a critical line of argument and justify a point of view, relating elements of their course of study to their broader context, as well as to specified aspects of human experience. Some of the tasks that appear below are designed to assist in developing those skills: teachers and students will doubtless think of others. It is important to remember at all times, however, to go beyond the simple facts about Judaism, which are relatively easy to learn, and to respond to all aspects of the religion in an open, empathetic and critically aware manner. Being able to appreciate different points of view is crucial in this regard.

This book and the accompanying teachers' book are constructed with Key Skills in mind. Students are asked to develop communication skills by taking part in discussions, gathering information and writing. They are asked to develop ICT skills through encouragement to make critically aware use of the Internet, and to present findings in the form of a project or dossier. They are asked to solve problems through making cases for particular viewpoints, and to work with others on joint research projects. They are also asked to reflect on their own learning and performance by using the self-assessment sheets provided in the teachers' book.

The students' and teachers' books both attempt to reflect the diversity of Judaism. Not only is this a requirement of the WJEC AS Specification, but it is also crucial to a proper, rounded understanding of the religion. All religious traditions contain a range of viewpoints and practices and students should be able to demonstrate a critical yet non-judgemental awareness of this fact. Teachers and students should take every opportunity to show the diversity of Judaism. To do otherwise is to risk a partial view of the religion, which could lead to unhelpful stereotyping.

As well as demonstrating awareness of the diversity of Judaism as a religion, students should also be able to demonstrate awareness that scholarly views of aspects of Judaism are diverse too. No one writer's view of a religion could be described as objective. Each writer brings to the study of Judaism their own unique view, including the writers of this text-book. Students should therefore be seeking to present the views of a number of writers. These views need not be classic arguments or philosophical positions, merely the way in which a writer presents certain aspects of the religion. This book should therefore be seen as just one book amongst many which contribute to the range of scholarly views on Judaism.

This book uses the abbreviations CE and BCE for Common Era and Before the Common Era. Some books use AD (Anno Domini) for CE and BC (Before Christ) for BCE. The actual years are the same, only the tag is different.

Section 1

Aim of the section

This section will ask you to evaluate the importance of the Law and other scriptural traditions in providing a foundation for Jewish belief and practice.

This means that you will need to consider:

1 **The structure and composition of the Torah and its role and authority in orthodox and non-orthodox Judaism.**

2 **The importance of revelation, covenant and of ethical monotheism in Judaism, and the role of the commandments in Jewish life.**

3 **The emergence of the rabbinic tradition, including the development of the Mishnah, Talmuds, Codes and Responsa.**

The foundations of Judaism

The foundation of the Jewish religion is the Law, the Torah. It is a key belief of the Jewish faith that the Torah came from God. It was given to the prophet Moses when he stood on Mount Sinai. The Book of Exodus describes what happened as follows: 'The people stood afar off, while Moses drew near to the thick darkness where God was. And the Lord said to Moses, "Thus you shall say to the people of Israel....These are the ordinances which you shall set before them"' (Exodus 20: 21-22. Chapter 21:1).

According to the tradition, Moses is a unique figure. He is said to be the only man in history with whom God used to speak familiarly. They used to speak 'face to face, as a man speaks to a friend' (Exodus 33:11). Thus God's words to Moses are the ultimate revelation and Orthodox Jews believe that these words are preserved intact in the first five books of the Scriptures, namely in Genesis, Exodus, Leviticus, Numbers and Deuteronomy. The twelfth century Jewish philosopher Maimonides insisted that this belief was an essential principle of the Jewish faith. As he put it: 'I believe with perfect faith that the whole and complete Torah as we now have it, is one and the same as that given to Moses...I believe that the Torah will never be changed, nor that any other law will be given in its place by the Creator.'

Over the centuries there have been many other prophets, wise men and teachers. They have also added to the Jewish tradition, but it is always stressed that their teachings are part of this God-given tradition which has its roots in the primary revelation to Moses. According to the Mishnah, the great collection of laws finally written down in the second century CE: 'Moses received the Torah on Mount Sinai and passed it on to Joshua, and Joshua to the elders, and the elders to the prophets and the prophets to the men of the Great Assembly...'

Law remains the foundation of the Jewish religion. It is written in the Mishnah that 'The World stands on three things - on the Torah, on the Temple service and on acts of kindness.' The Temple was destroyed in 70CE so there are no longer Temple services. However the Torah and acts of kindness survive as the twin pillars of the whole system. It is an ancient tradition and, for religious Jews, one that is as relevant today as it was in ancient times.

'All the things that happened in the wilderness are repeated in history. You see the same things now - the census, looking for a leader, people grizzling. It doesn't mean that because you're a good leader you'll get to see the result. Moses was denied the chance to lead his people into the Promised Land even though he was their leader.'

Norma, Swansea

Time Line

- **c.1280 BCE – the Exodus (although this date is debated by scholars)**
- **c. 1000 BCE – Jerusalem becomes capital of the nation under David**
- **c. 967 BCE - beginning of Solomon's reign and the construction of the Temple**
- **722 BCE – Assyrians conquer Northern Kingdom (Israel)**
- **586 BCE – Babylonians conquer Southern Kingdom (Judah) and destroy the Temple, taking the Jewish elite into exile**
- **538 BCE – Cyrus the Great of Persia permits the return of the exiles**
- **516 BCE – dedication of the Second Temple**
- **164 BCE – rededication of the Temple after the Maccabean revolt**
- **70 CE – destruction of the Second Temple under the Roman General Titus**
- **c.200 CE – the Mishnah of Judah haNasi**
- **c.500 CE - completion of the Babylonian Talmud**
- **d. 1204 - Moses Maimonides**
- **c 1810 – Reform movement begins in Germany**
- **1844 – the Orthodox movement separates itself from Progressive Judaism**
- **1938- Kristallnacht, destruction of Jewish synagogues and beginning of the Holocaust**
- **1948 – creation of the State of Israel**

Chapter 1

The Hebrew Scriptures

Aim

After studying this chapter you should be able to demonstrate clear knowledge and understanding of the structure of the Torah, the uniqueness of revelation in Judaism, and the importance of the Torah in worship. You should be able to evaluate the different interpretations made of the Law by Orthodox and non-Orthodox Jews, and you should be able to comment on questions about the authority of the Torah for Jewish life and practice. You should be able to demonstrate your knowledge and understanding of the role of the 613 ritual and moral laws (mitzvot), and to show that you have reflected on implications of the belief that these have divine authority for Jews.

The Hebrew Scriptures contain the same books as the Christian Old Testament. Some tell the story of the history of the Jewish people. Some are works of prophecy; they give God's will. There are also law books as well as collections of poetry and sayings. Traditionally the Jews have divided the collection into three. The first six books are known in Hebrew as Torah (literally law); the second group, which includes the history books of Joshua, Judges, Samuel and Kings as well as all the prophetic books, is described collectively as Prophecy (Neviim); and the final, more miscellaneous selection, is called Writings (Ketuvim). Collectively, the whole is known as the Tenakh - an acronym based on the first letters of the three groups.

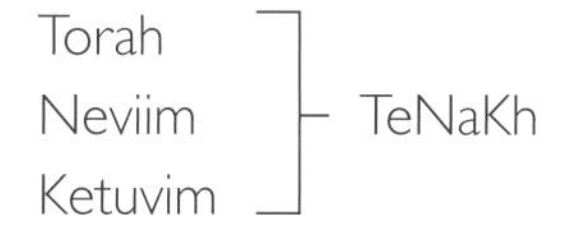

The nature of the Tenakh

Traditionally Jews have made an important division between the books of Torah and the rest of the Tenakh. It is a fundamental article of the Jewish faith that the first five books of the Hebrew Scriptures were given intact by God to Moses on Mount Sinai. Thus they have a particular and a unique authority. They are literally the word of God. Although the Prophets and the Writings were also thought to be divinely inspired, they did not have the same direct authority.

This is not to say the other books are unimportant. The Book of Genesis describes how God made a promise to Abraham, the forefather of the Jewish people. He said, 'I will make of you a great nation, and I will bless you and make your name great' (Genesis 12: 2-3). Later, the Book of Deuteronomy describes the way in which the Jews have a special relationship with God. 'The Lord has chosen you out of all the peoples on earth to be his people, his treasured possession' (Deuteronomy 7: 6). The Neviim, the books of history and prophecy, are a record of how that divine promise was kept.

Torah scrolls displayed (18th century engraving).

Orthodox Jews consider the Torah to be the word of God. How does this affect their treatment of the scrolls?

Religious Jews understood their history as demonstrating God's activity in their lives. Underlying the text is the constant theme that God is faithful to his promise as long as the Jews keep their side of the bargain. If they are obedient to Him, God will protect them and preserve them in the Land of Israel. If, however, they turn away, forget his Torah and worship other gods, disaster is the inevitable consequence. The people are conquered, they are enslaved and sent into exile. Again and again the prophets warn of disasters to come. Again and again the people fail to mend their ways and it is left to the historians to demonstrate how the Jews' enemies have triumphed.

The books of the Neviim and the Ketuvim

The Book of Joshua is the first of the history books in the Neviim. Joshua took over the leadership after the death of Moses and he led the people to the Promised Land. The Book of Judges describes how the Jews defended themselves against their enemies in the early days. The Books of Samuel and Kings explain why they felt it was necessary to have a king, but how eventually they were conquered by the Assyrians in 721BCE and the Babylonians in 586BCE. The earliest of the writing prophets, Amos, probably dates from the eighth century BCE and the latest, perhaps Malachi, from the fifth century. Thus the Neviim cover a period of approximately eight hundred years and consist of both a chronicle and a commentary on historical events.

The Ketuvim are different and do not share a single theme. The Psalms are a collection of poems dedicated to God. Lamentations are a group of five poems mourning the destruction of Jerusalem by the Babylonians. Ecclesiastes offers a particular philosophy of life. Proverbs is an anthology of short sayings and the Song of Songs is an extended love poem. The Book of Job is an attempt to understand why the righteous suffer, and the Books of Ruth, Esther and Daniel contain important legends. I and II Chronicles is another version of Jewish history and Ezra and Nehemiah refer to the period when the Jews had returned to the Promised Land after their exile in Babylon.

The Books of the Tenakh are by no means the only books that were written by the Jews of ancient times. We know there were others because they are mentioned in the Biblical text: 'Now the rest of the acts of Jeroboam...behold they are written in the Chronicles of the Kings of Israel' (I Kings 14:19). We do not know why these particular books survived while others were lost. Nor do we know how they came to be regarded as authoritative. Nonetheless, the final decisions had been agreed by the middle of the second century CE and some of the books date from at least a thousand years before that.

The authority of the Torah

The question of the authority of the Torah is one that divides the modern Jewish community. As we have seen, it was an essential article of faith that these five books were literally dictated by God to Moses. Therefore every word must be true. Altogether there are six hundred and thirteen commandments (Hebrew – 'mitzvot') in the Torah. Two hundred and forty-eight are positive, (such as 'Be fruitful and multiply' or 'Observe the Sabbath day and keep it holy,') and three hundred and sixty-five are negative, ('You shall not boil a kid in its mother's milk' and 'You shall not bear false witness' i.e. 'You shall not lie'). Altogether the six hundred and thirteen cover every aspect of everyday life and also include a number of ritual mitzvot concerning religious worship. Best known are the Ten Commandments found in Exodus 20 and again in Deuteronomy 5. These include four ritual laws and ten moral ones.

It must be stressed that the Ten Commandments are no more important that the other six hundred and three. Similarly the ritual mitzvot should be taken as seriously as the moral ones. The reason for obeying them is not because society will be happier if it is well-ordered or because they encourage sensible hygiene or a stable family life. Traditionally Jews believe that the law should be kept because that is what God demands. There is no other justification. It must also be stressed that Jews do not expect non-Jews to keep all the mitzvot. The Torah is for the Jewish people alone and it is the token of their special relationship with God (See Chapter 2).

Seminar topic

Why are the ritual laws as important as the moral laws in Judaism?

Who, or what, do you think is the ultimate source of authority for human behaviour? God? Scripture? Human beings?

Questions of authorship

However most modern scholarship has called into question Moses' authorship of the Torah. For many years it has been recognised that stories are repeated and that there are obvious differences of style within the text. The first chapter of the story of Joseph (Genesis 37) illustrates this clearly. In some verses Joseph's father is called Jacob, but in some verses he is known as Israel. The brothers sometimes hate Joseph because of his dreams but sometimes because he is their father's favourite. In one place it seems to be Reuben who tries to save Joseph, but in another it is Judah and it is not clear whether Joseph is sold to Midianite or Ishmaelite traders. The obvious explanation for these differences is that the text comes from two different sources. But if that is so, then it cannot have been dictated directly by God.

Among most biblical scholars today there is a general agreement that the first five books of the Hebrew Scriptures (known as the Pentateuch, which is Greek for 'Five Books') are a collection of traditions, all composed at different times. Inevitably, many Jews have come to share this opinion. Some have abandoned their faith altogether, but many continue to hold the Torah in great reverence. At the same time they no longer see it as completely authoritative. Such Jews are generally described as non-Orthodox. In the United States the main non-Orthodox groups are known as Conservative and Reform. Both have their own religious organisations and synagogues. In Great Britain parallel non-Orthodox groups are the Reform and the Liberal.

Questions of interpretation

All the non-Orthodox feel free to interpret Jewish law in accordance with modern customs and understanding. There are countless examples of the differences between Orthodox and non-Orthodox interpretations of Jewish Law. For example, in the case of a failed marriage, the Torah declares that if a man wishes to divorce his wife he must give her a proper document of divorce (Deuteronomy 24:1). There is no parallel way for a woman to release herself from a cruel or abusive husband. The American Conservative movement has avoided the problem by writing into all marriage contracts that a marriage is automatically annulled if a husband refuses unreasonably to give his wife a divorce. The Reform movement has declared the ancient law unfair and ignores the law altogether.

Meanwhile the Orthodox continue to practise their religion in the traditional manner. They do not accept the findings of modern scholarship and therefore continue to regard the Torah as infallible, or perfectly correct and true. This means that they live their lives strictly in accordance with the law (See Chapters 5-10) and they are unwavering in their disapproval of the non-Orthodox. Although they form only a small proportion of the Jewish people, they continue to exert an influence far beyond their numerical strength. This is partly because they are regarded with awe by other Jews and partly because they are in control of all the official religious organisations in the State of Israel. In Great Britain, the biggest synagogue organisation, led by the Chief Rabbi, is Orthodox. This does not mean that most British Jews live their lives as Orthodox Jews. They just prefer to support an Orthodox rather than a non-Orthodox religious organisation.

Tasks

The following extract is from a formal statement of non-orthodox Jewish belief, called the Columbus Platform, written in America in 1937 by the Reform Jewish community.

'Revelation is a continuous process, confined not to one group and to no one age. Yet the people of Israel, through its prophets and sages, achieved unique insight into the realm of religious truth. The Torah, both written and oral, enshrines Israel's ever-growing consciousness of God and of the moral law. It preserves the historical precedents, sanctions and norms of Jewish life, and seeks to mould it in the patterns of goodness and holiness. **Being products of historical processes, certain of its laws have lost their binding force with the passing of the conditions which called them forth**. But as a depository of permanent spiritual ideals, the Torah remains the dynamic source of the life of Israel. Each age has the obligation to adapt the teachings of the Torah to its basic needs in consonance with the genius of Judaism.'

From Nicholas De Lange, *Judaism*, OUP, 1986

Writing task	Explain the meaning of the sentence in bold.

The following is a statement by an important Orthodox Rabbi, Samson Raphael Hirsch 1808-88.

'If the Bible is to be for me the word of God, and Judaism and the Jewish law the revealed will of God, am I to be allowed to take my stand on the highway of the ages and the lands and ask every mortal pilgrim on earth for his opinions, born as they are between dream and waking, between error and truth, in order to submit the word of the living God to his approval, in order to mould it to suit his passing whim? Am I to say: 'See here modern, purified Judaism! Here we have the word of the living God, refined, approved and purified by men!'

From W. Oxtoby (Ed), 'The Dangers of Updating Judaism' quoted in *World Religions: Western Traditions*, OUP, 1996 p127

Writing tasks	
	Explain the consequences for religious practice of believing that the Torah is not infallible.
	To what extent is the non-Orthodox interpretation of scripture justified?

Seminar topic
Who wrote the Pentateuch?
What are the main differences in the attitudes summarised in the readings above?

The use of the Tenakh

Although the Tenakh is printed for home and synagogue use in a single volume, the Torah continues to be written out by hand in the sacred language of Hebrew on huge parchment scrolls. Every synagogue has at least one of these scrolls and it is the focus of synagogue worship. It is kept in the Ark, a large ornate cupboard in the eastern wall of the building. When the doors of the Ark are opened and the scroll is taken out or put back, the congregation stands as a sign of respect. This is an acknowledgement of the central role of the Torah in Jewish life and it is considered an honour to be asked to open or close the doors.

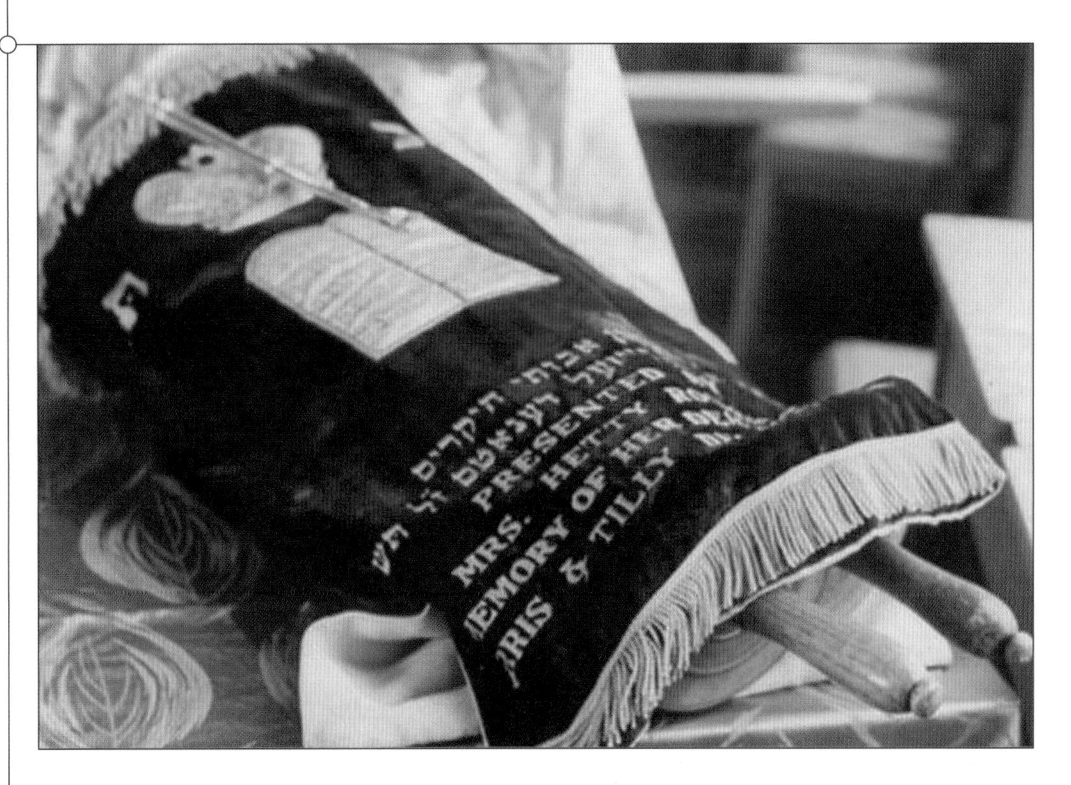

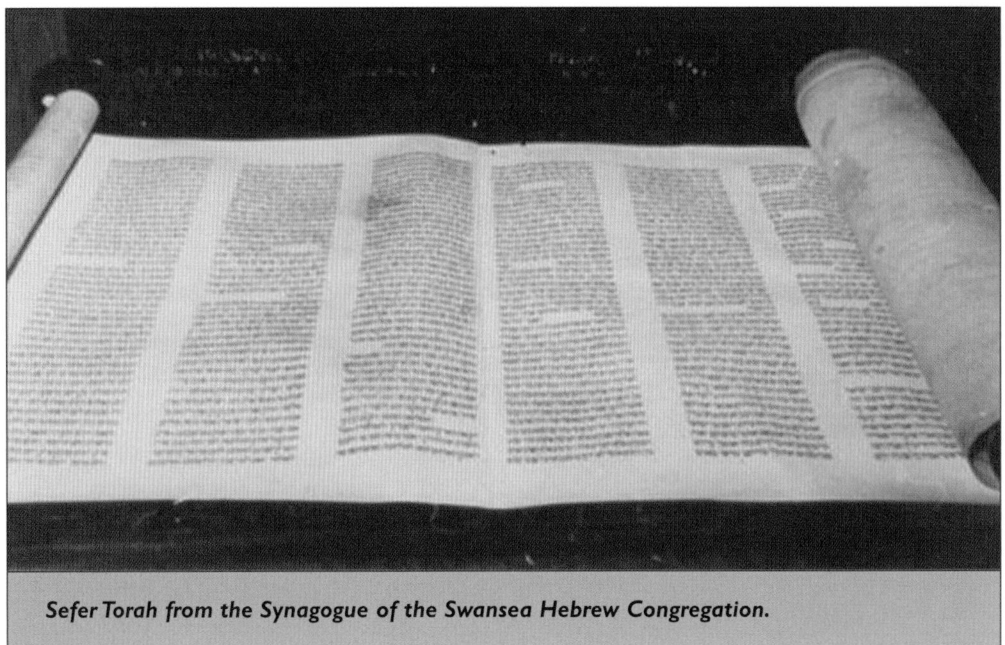

Sefer Torah from the Synagogue of the Swansea Hebrew Congregation.

The scroll itself ('Sefer Torah') is often an object of great beauty. The lengths of parchment are sewn together to form a long roll. Each end is attached to a wooden stave and when it is not in use it is kept rolled up in an elaborately decorated cover. The cover can be of carved wood or of embroidered cloth. Over the cover is placed a silver decoration, reminiscent of the silver breastplate worn by the high priest in ancient times.

Silver decorations on the Sefer Torah in the Synagogue of the Swansea Hebrew Congregation.

Crowns on the Sefer Torah in the Synagogue of the Swansea Hebrew Congregation.

Can you explain why Sefer Torah are decorated like this?

On the tops of the wooden staves are fitted silver decorations, often in the form of crowns to show that the Torah rules the life of the Jewish community.

When the scroll is unfurled, the reader uses a silver pointer, called a yad, so that the text will not be dirtied by human fingers.

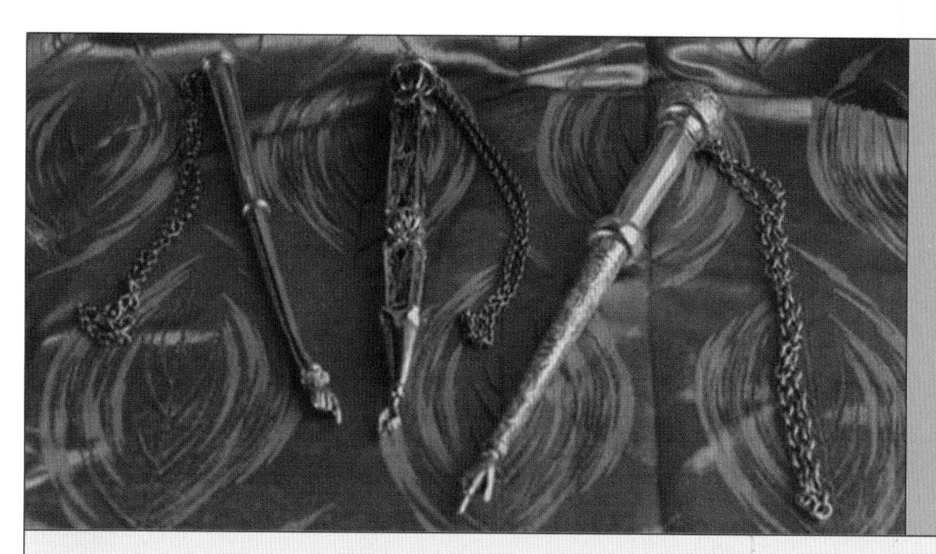

Yads in the Synagogue of the Swansea Hebrew Congregation.

'When you read from the Sefer Torah, the pointers help you follow the words, because you mustn't touch the text with your hands. It's difficult for an inexperienced person to read from the Sefer Torah because there are no vowels.'

David, Swansea

Sefer Torah and yad.

Why would it be unacceptable for human fingers to touch the scroll?

The Torah in worship

Over the course of a year, the entire Torah is read aloud in the synagogue. The text is divided into set weekly portions and the annual cycle begins and ends on the Festival of the Rejoicing in the Law, (see Chapter 6). Every Sabbath, the Torah is carried out from the Ark with considerable ceremony and the congregation bows as it goes past. It is read from a central platform in the building so that everyone can hear it. Traditionally every Sabbath seven readers are called up in turn. Each one recites a blessing and then the rabbi or official leader of the service reads the prescribed passage from the scroll. In Orthodox synagogues only men are invited, but in non-Orthodox synagogues women can also have this role. The non-Orthodox movements also ordain women as rabbis.

The words of the service, many of which come from the Psalms, emphasise the importance of the Torah in Jewish life: 'Blessed be He who gave the Torah to His people Israel in His holiness. The Torah of the Lord is perfect, refreshing the soul...And this is the Torah which Moses put before the Children of Israel as commanded by the Lord...It is the tree of life to those who grasp it and those who hold it are truly happy. Its ways are ways of pleasantness and all its paths are peace.'

After the Torah reading is over, another scriptural passage is always read. This is known as the Haftarah ('conclusion') and can come from any part of the Neviim or the Ketuvim. Again the passage is prescribed and it is chosen because it provides some sort of commentary on, or is in some way connected to, the Torah passage. Particular readings are also connected with particular festivals, for example the Book of Ruth is read on the festival of Shavu'ot (see Chapter 6) and the Book of Jonah on Yom Kippur (see Chapter 8).

'I feel there is a special connection between the Welsh and Hebrew languages. The Welsh have struggled over the years to keep their language alive. It has been the same with the Jewish people. Hebrew was the language of prayer for the Jewish people all over the world, but like Latin, it was a 'dead' language - a language which was read in prayer but not spoken as a means of everyday communication. However when the State of Israel was formed Hebrew was revived as a modern spoken language. It is no longer a 'dead' language but is the official language spoken by Israelis today. Many Welsh people have said that it was the Welsh hymns, several of which are based on Jewish psalms and thoughts, and the translation of the Hebrew scriptures into Welsh, which helped the Welsh language to survive.'

Rosalind, Swansea

At home, passages from the Tenakh are used for greeting the Sabbath (see Chapter 5) and at festivals such as Pesach (Passover) and Sukkot (Tabernacles) (see Chapter 6) and Purim (Lots) (see Chapter 7). All Jewish children are expected to learn some Hebrew so that they can read the Tenakh aloud in its original language and can understand the prayers in the synagogue. Through reading the Hebrew text of the Tenakh and the prayer book, the Jew remains in touch with the old traditions. Wherever a Jew may go in the world, he or she will understand the readings and prayers and will share a common heritage with all fellow Jews, whatever their background or nationality.

This leaf comes from the Book of Jonah in the Neviim.

Glossary

Ark	Niche in the synagogue in which the Sefer Torah are kept. In Biblical times the container which held the tablets of the law, carried by the Israelites in the wilderness, and installed in the Holy of Holies in the Temple.
Hebrew	The Semitic language in which most of the Jewish scriptures are written.
Infallible	When Orthodox Jews describe the Torah as infallible, they mean that every word is a revelation from God, there is no human interpretation involved and deviating in any way from any of the teachings in it is breaking the covenant. In other words, the written Torah is a perfectly accurate and complete record of God's revelation.
Mishnah	The oral law, compiled and written down in the second century by Judah haNasi, and divided into six sections or sedarim. The oral law was believed to have been given to Moses at the same time as the written law, and was passed on and explained and commented upon through the generations.
Mitzvot	Commandments or obligations (sing. Mitzvah). There are 613 mitzvot, which were given to the Jews in Exodus, and compliance with these commandments is central to Orthodox Jewish life.
Sabbath	In Hebrew, 'Shabbat'. The seventh day of the week (sunset Friday till sunset Saturday), during which Jews must abstain from work.
Sefer Torah	The scroll on which the Pentateuch is written. Sefer Torah are stored in the Ark, in the wall of the synagogue facing Jerusalem.
Tenakh	Also spelt 'Tanak'. An abbreviation of the first letters of the three Hebrew words that designate the sections of the Hebrew Bible: Torah, Neviim and Ketuvim. The Tenakh is therefore, the Hebrew Bible.
The Promised Land	The land of Canaan, promised to Abraham and his descendants as part of the Covenant.
Torah	Literally 'teaching'. The strict sense of the word torah is reserved for the laws inPentateuch. The term is also used for the first five books collectively, and also to refer to the whole of Jewish teachings, contained both in the Hebrew Bible and in the Oral Law.

Significant themes in the Tenakh

Aim

After studying this chapter you should be able to demonstrate clear knowledge and understanding of the role and significance in Judaism of the relationship between God and humans, as expressed through the account of creation in Genesis, and through the notion of Covenant. The chapter asks you explore the implications for Jews of belief in One God who created the world, who commands his people and brings about historical events. You should be able to comment on the Jewish understanding of chosenness as responsibility as well as privilege, and the relationship of the Jewish people to the rest of the world.

The Tenakh includes a variety of different books and a corresponding variety of themes. Nonetheless the Hebrew Scriptures offer a unified and highly influential view of human history.

Ethical monotheism

The Tenakh teaches that the universe was created by God and that God is personally concerned with the destiny of both individuals and nations. He is particularly concerned with the fate of his Chosen People, the Jews, who will ultimately bring all peoples into a proper relationship with God. The Jewish Scriptures also emphasise that God wants social justice throughout the earth and that His law is the platform on which civilised human society should rest.

This view is commonly known as ethical monotheism, that is, the belief in One God who is the source of all morality. The 'oneness' of God is a particularly important feature of ethical monotheism, and Jews are constantly reminded of their relationship to the one God in the Shema: 'Hear O Israel, the Lord our God the Lord is One' (Deuteronomy 6: 4). This means that God has no helpers, relations, or rivals, and it is one of the reasons there is a strong prohibition (ban) in Judaism on making images of God. Worshipping an image would be worshipping something other than God, thus suggesting he has a rival and compromising his oneness. It also means that he alone is responsible for everything that happens in the world. This means that when bad things happen, Jews have an obligation to accept and to seek meaning in them, often requiring them to reflect upon the role their own behaviour played in prompting God to act in particular ways.

Some Names of God in Jewish Tradition

YHWH (The Tetragramaton) -	The Lord (also, *Adonai, Yah*)
El, Eloha, Elohim -	God
Shaddai -	Almighty
Ha-Kadosh Barukh Hu -	The Holy One, Blessed be He
Ribono Shel Olam -	Master of the Universe
Ha-Makom -	The Place
Ha-Rahman -	The Merciful
Shekhinah -	The Divine Presence
En-Sof -	The Infinite
Gevurah -	The All-strong
Tsur Yisrael -	Rock of Israel
Shomer Yisrael -	Guardian of Israel
Melekh Malkhé Melakhim -	The Supreme King of Kings

It is clear from the Tenakh that God requires particular behaviour from his people, since he commands them to act in particular ways. However, ethical monotheism is about much more than merely following commandments. The Ketuvim tell of people struggling to live life righteously, imitating the goodness of God, and acting in such a way as to conform to the order that is obviously present in God's creation. It is also about seeing all aspects of life as having an inseparable relationship with God. God's oneness is not merely one amongst his qualities; it means that he is the source of everything and the destination of everything. His creation is not somehow separate from him; it is in a relationship of unity with him.

Jews have never formed more than a tiny percentage of the world's population, but their religious influence has been enormous. The founder of Christianity, Jesus of Nazareth, was himself a Jew and the Tenakh was adopted as the Old Testament by his followers. Judaism was also important in the thinking of Muhammad, the prophet of Islam. Through these two daughter-religions, the teachings of the Jews about ethical monotheism have spread throughout the world.

Tasks

Writing tasks	
	Explain what Jews mean by the belief that God is the source of all morality.
	'Without religion there is no morality. It is everyone for themselves.' Assess the validity of this view.
	Explain why Jews emphasise that God is 'One.'
	'Monotheism is superior to polytheism (belief in many gods).' Assess the validity of this view.

God the Creator

The first book of the Tenakh, the Book of Genesis, teaches that God is the source of the whole universe. The first chapter reads, 'In the beginning, God created the heavens and the earth. The earth was without form and void and darkness was upon the face of the deep: and the Spirit of God was moving over the face of the waters. And God said, "Let there be light;" and there was light...' The text goes on to explain how God worked for six days. He created the heavens, the seas and the dry land. He caused vegetation of every kind to grow in the earth. He made the sun, the moon and the stars and he brought into being all the fish, birds, insects and animals. Finally he created human beings to rule over the earth's creatures.

The second chapter also emphasises that God made everything, but suggests that God made man before He made the plants and the trees. Then He decided that man needed companionship, so first he created the animals and birds and then finally He made woman. In both cases human beings are regarded as the crown of God's creation. The Scriptures also emphasise that God continues to be closely involved in the world He has made. As the writer of Psalm 89 put it: 'O Lord God of Hosts, who is as mighty as you, O Lord? … You rule the raging sea; when its waves rise, you still them…the heavens are yours, the earth is also yours' (8-9, 11). So every change in the atmosphere, every new leaf and every fresh birth, is evidence of the ongoing process of God's creation. The Tenakh teaches that God is both transcendent (high above all human understanding) and immanent (close at hand). On the one hand, in the Book of Isaiah, God declares: 'My thoughts are not your thoughts, neither are your ways my ways....For as the heavens are higher than the earth, so are my ways higher than your ways and my thoughts higher than your thoughts' (Isiah 55: 8-9). At the same time the writer of Psalm 139 can ask: 'Where can I go from your spirit? Or where can I flee from your presence? If I ascend to heaven you are there; if I make my bed in Sheol ('the underworld'), you are there. If I take the wings of the morning and settle at the farthest limits of the sea, even there your hand shall lead me' (7-10).

The nature of God

Thus the Tenakh stresses that God is outside and beyond the universe He has made, but at the same time, He is closely involved in its every detail. Nor is He morally neutral. The Creation story constantly repeats that God saw that his work was good (Genesis 1: 4, 10, 12, 18, 21, 25). The creation is a reflection of His own nature. It is good because He himself is good. As the author of Psalm 145 put it: 'The Lord is gracious and merciful, slow to anger and abounding in steadfast love. The Lord is good to all, and his compassion is over all that He has made' (8-9). If God has put human beings in charge of the earth, then they too should exercise their rule with love and compassion. As God's partners in the creative process, they have the responsibility for growing food, for protecting God's creatures and for developing natural resources. And they too should see that their work is good.

Seminar topic

To say that God is both transcendent and immanent is a paradox.

What does this mean? How can both descriptions of God's relationship with humans be true?

Questions of creation and evolution

This traditional picture of creation has been called into question by modern science. Darwin's theory of evolution suggests that human beings evolved over an immense period of time from other creatures. Although they are the most intelligent entities to have so far developed, there is no essential difference between human beings and other animals. Most religious people are not disturbed by this. Without putting aside or ignoring scientific explanations, it is still possible to see the goodness of God in the natural world and to feel strongly that preserving the beauty and fruitfulness of the earth is humanity's responsibility.

The Covenant

One essential element of the Jewish faith is that the Jews are the chosen people of God. The Torah recounts a series of agreements made by God with individuals. Most significantly he charges Abraham, the first of the Patriarchs, to keep his law, the reward for which is that Abraham's descendants (i.e. the Jews) will prosper in the land of Canaan. The Book of Deuteronomy teaches: 'You are a people holy to the Lord your God; the Lord your God has chosen you to be a people for His own possession out of all the peoples that are on the face of the earth' (Deuteronomy 7:6). The text goes on to explain that the Jews were not chosen because they were the most numerous or significant group. Rather it was because 'the Lord loves you and is keeping His oath which He swore to your forefather'

Seminar topic

Can the Genesis account of creation be reconciled with the findings of modern science about the origins of the world and of human life?

(Verse 8). The role of the Jewish people is also spelled out in the Book of Exodus: 'If you will obey my voice...you shall be my own possession among all peoples...you shall be for me a kingdom of priests and a holy nation' (Exodus19: 5-6).

Penalties and privileges

It is important to emphasise that God's choice does not mean that the Jews will be indiscriminately favoured. Since Jews believe that they are in a covenant relationship, it carries huge responsibility. A covenant is a two-sided bargain that has been freely entered into by both parties and it carries penalties as well as privileges. The people will only be chosen if they continue to keep God's commandments. If they are disobedient and turn away from God, then disaster will befall the nation.

Alan Segal explains that covenant ('berith') is 'the central organising concept in Israelite religion. It is a theological term that means much the same thing that "contract" does today. The purpose of life is defined by the special contractual relationship into which Abraham, Isaac, Jacob, and Moses enter with God. The covenant specifies exactly which human behaviours God wants and which he does not. It gives a divine mandate to their societal laws.'
W. Oxtoby (Ed), *World Religions: Western Traditions*, p23.

'No Jew can tell another Jew how to live. We are responsible for ourselves. The good Jew is the one who sets the example, the one who 'lives' it. If someone sets an example to others, it makes me want to emulate it, and I know I fall short.'

David, Swansea

Stained glass window in the Synagogue in Swansea, showing the twelve tribes.

Modern Jews have a strong sense of the past: is this reasonable?

The Book of Exodus goes on to describe how Moses read the Book of the Covenant to the people. After he had finished, the people saw what was entailed and they accepted their duties. They declared: 'All that the Lord has spoken we will do, and we will be obedient' (Exodus 24: 7). During the course of Jewish history, however, the people frequently did turn away from God. Again and again the prophets warned of the dire consequences of their behaviour. Writing in the eighth century BCE, Hosea described God's rejection of the Jews: 'The Lord said: Call his name Not-My-People, for you are not my people and I am not your God' (Hosea 1: 9).

In 721BCE, the ten northern tribes of the people were overrun by the Assyrian army. They were taken into exile; there they intermarried with the surrounding peoples and their special identity was lost forever. Only two of the twelve tribes remained.

Despite this visible proof of God's abandonment, the prophets could not believe that God would give up his chosen people entirely. Hosea himself, drawing on his own experience of an unhappy marriage, insisted that God would forgive his people again and again. God says: 'How can I give you up O Ephraim; how can I hand you over O Israel...My heart recoils within me, my compassion grows warm and tender' (Hosea 11:12). Even today pious Jews (Jews who carefully keep all the commandments and try to live good lives) would agree. Despite a terrible history of exile and persecution, which culminated in Hitler's murder of six million in the Holocaust, the Jewish people have survived. They continue to offer their unique religious vision to the world.

Nazi soldiers clearing the Warsaw ghetto during the Second World War.

Why might some people find it difficult to believe in a compassionate God when there is so much suffering in the world?

Living with chosenness

Nonetheless the Jews themselves have not always been comfortable with the idea of chosenness. A story circulated that the privilege was offered to all the other nations first. Each in turn rejected it because they did not want to keep God's Torah. Only after God threatened imminent destruction were the Jews, the least of all peoples, prepared to turn away from their old ways and be obedient to the commandments. There is an old joke that considering all the disasters that have occurred in the Jews' long history, perhaps it is time God chose someone else!

Certainly, the doctrine has not made the Jews popular in the outside world. Almost from its beginning, the Christian Church has taught that the Jews have forfeited their special position since they have rejected Jesus as their Messiah. Instead, Christianity teaches that the Church is the new chosen Israel of God. Among anti-Semites (people who are prejudiced against Jews), the doctrine has resulted in the Jews being accused of racism. They argue that it implies that the Jews think they are superior to everyone else. This negative view is perhaps best summarised by the English poet Hilaire Belloc who wrote: 'How odd of God, to choose the Jews!' The only response to this can be the anonymous reply: 'It isn't odd! The Jews chose God!'

Tasks

Writing tasks	Explain and illustrate the Jewish belief in chosenness.
	'Jews see their chosenness as a responsibility and not a privilege.' How accurate is this statement?
Research task	Compile a summary of the Biblical sources for belief in chosenness.

Sanctification of history

The Torah as a whole is seen as an account of God's activities within history, starting from the point of the creation of the world. For example, the liberation from Egypt reported in Exodus, is not just a historical event; it is sanctified, or holy, because God brought it about. God's actions are seen through his relationship with his people, the Jews, and these actions have implications for all other peoples.

As we have seen, the Book of Exodus has God promise that the Jews will be a 'kingdom of priests' (Exodus 19:6). The Jewish people themselves have understood this to mean that they have a mission to bring the knowledge of the one true God to the world. They do not expect non-Jews to obey all the six hundred and thirteen laws of the Torah. Those commandments are for Jews alone. For everyone else it is enough to keep a few basic moral rules, such as avoiding murder, incest, adultery and idolatry. At the same time, the Torah is understood as the blueprint for everything that exists.
In the Book of Proverbs, one of the books of the Ketuvim section of the Tenakh, Divine Wisdom is described as having an essential role in the creation of the universe: 'The Lord by wisdom founded the earth; by understanding he established the heavens; by his knowledge the deeps broke forth, and the clouds drop down the dew' (Proverbs 3:19), and 'When He marked out the foundations of the earth, then I was beside Him like a master workman: and I was daily his delight, rejoicing before Him always...And now, my children, listen to me: happy are those who keep my ways' (Proverbs 8: 29-30, 32). Traditionally the Torah has been identified as that divine wisdom.

Thus the Torah has cosmic significance. 'Law' is far too narrow a translation. The word should be understood as 'instruction', 'teaching' or even 'pattern'. By the first century CE, the rabbis were teaching that long before the creation of the universe, the Torah lay in God's bosom and sang his praises with the angels. It was thought that, not only was the Torah an account of all God's actions in history, but that God consulted the Torah before embarking on the whole process of the creation and it was an active instrument in the making of the world.

Waiting for the Messiah

Connected with this idea that human history is linked to God's actions, is the conviction that God will send a Messiah, a new king, who will gather the Jewish people back from exile and who will establish truth and justice forever. The prophet Ezekiel described these future events: 'Thus says the Lord God: Behold I will take the people of Israel from the nations among which they have gone...they shall be my people and I shall be their God. My servant David will be king over them...I will make a covenant of peace with them...Then the nations will know that I the Lord sanctify Israel, when my sanctuary is among them forevermore' (Ezekiel 37:21-28).

Stained glass window in the Synagogue in Swansea, showing the Star of David.

It is obvious that this happy state of affairs has not yet come into being. This is why the Jews do not believe that Jesus of Nazareth, along with many other claimants, was God's promised Messiah. Today pious Jews are still waiting. Others have abandoned the hope. The Zionist movement (which supports the modern State of Israel) transformed the religious promise into a political campaign for the establishment of a national homeland for the Jewish people. In the 19th Century, the Reform movement rejected the idea of a Messiah. Instead they looked forward to a universal golden age, when, through the advances of science and through social reform, the world would be perfected by human beings. Despite these differences of opinion, Jews are agreed that there is still much to be done. In every synagogue service they pray for a time when 'The Lord shall be king over all the earth; in that day the Lord shall be One and his name One.'

The Jewish mission to the world

The Jewish people are the custodians of the Torah and, as such, have a particular mission to the world. Through their faithfulness to God's commandments, they testify to the reality of God. Ultimately they believe that this testimony will transform everything. The prophet Isaiah described the final enlightenment of all the peoples of the world: ' In days to come the mountain of the Lord's house shall be established as the highest of the mountains, and shall be raised above the hills; all nations shall stream to it. Many peoples shall come and say, "Come let us go up to the mountain of the Lord, to the house of the God of Jacob; that He may teach us his ways and that we may walk in his paths." For out of Zion shall go forth the law, and the word of the Lord from Jerusalem. He shall judge between the nations, and he shall decide for many peoples; and they shall beat their swords into ploughshares, and their spears into pruning hooks; nation shall not lift up sword against nation, neither shall they learn war any more' (Isaiah 2: 2-4).

Seminar topic

Were the Jews right to reject the messiah-ship of Jesus?

Tasks

Research task	Collect and comment on cuttings from newspapers and evidence from Internet sites that illustrate the belief of some Jews that campaigning for the modern state of Israel is helping to fulfil the Biblical covenant.
Writing tasks	Explain the Jewish understanding of the covenant. Evaluate the view that Jewish faithfulness to the covenant has benefits for all.

Glossary

Chosen People	The belief that the Jews were chosen by God to have a special mission and responsibility.
Chosenness	Covenant 'promise', the special relationship between God and his people the Jews, stated a number of times, in different ways. In brief the covenant requires the Jews to keep the commandments, and to make the sign of the covenant by circumcising their eight day old boys, and in return God promises the Land of Israel to the people.
Idolatry	The sin of worshipping an image, a person, or anything which is not God. In Judaism the worship of any God other than the God of Israel.
Immanent	The presence of God in the world and in nature.
Messiah	A King or great leader who, it is prophesied, will bring the Jews back to Israel and rule them there according to God's laws.
Polytheism	The belief in many gods. Canaanite religion was polytheistic. Judaism is resolutely monotheistic.
Reform movement	A movement originating in the 19th century which encouraged the Jews living in the diaspora (outside Israel) to become fully functioning members of the societies in which they were living, and to take a modernist approach to the scriptures. As such, many Reform Jews do not keep all 613 of the mitzvot.
Sanctification	'To make holy'. Jews believe that history is sanctified by the actions of God within it.
Transcendent	God as above and beyond the world and nature, as beyond human understanding, as superior to all the created world.
Zion	The name of one of the hills in Jerusalem, the word Zion came to mean the whole of ancient Israel, as the promised land.

Mishnah and Midrash

Aim

After studying this chapter you should be able to demonstrate clear knowledge and understanding of the impact of the destruction of the Second temple on Judaism. You should be able to comment on the importance of scholarship, legal debate and the Oral Law in the survival of Judaism. You should also be able to evaluate the importance of the Mishnah, with its Six Orders, the Tosefta and the Midrash in the emerging Rabbinic tradition, and in Judaism today.

In the 1st Century CE, the Promised Land was part of the vast Roman Empire. In 70CE the Jews rebelled against the Roman overlords and, during the ensuing war, the Temple in Jerusalem was destroyed and the Jews were scattered.

The Arch of Titus, showing Roman soldiers looting the Jerusalem Temple.

Consider the impact on Judaism of the destruction of the Temple in 70CE.

This was an unimaginable catastrophe. No longer could daily sacrifices take place. Nor was there a central place of pilgrimage in the Jewish world. With the Temple a burnt-out ruin, Judaism could all too easily have disappeared as did so many of the religions of the ancient world. It survived this event, known as the Dispersion, because it adapted itself to the new circumstances.

Already many Jews were living outside the land of Israel. They had organised communal schools and places of worship known as synagogues. These buildings became the focus of the local community. The Scriptures could be read, studied and discussed; children were instructed and regular services (without sacrifices) were held. Even though the Temple had been destroyed, groups of scholars, the Tannaim, (literally 'repeaters') continued to come together. They formed academies in which they concentrated on the development of the legal tradition and on the precise meaning of the words of the Bible. Ultimately, in the third century CE this was to produce the Mishnah and the Midrash.

Seminar topic

Suggest some reasons why Judaism survived after the Dispersion.

The nature of the Mishnah

The Mishnah is the record of the legal discussions which took place in these academies while rabbinic interpretation of the Tenakh is known as Midrash. Through these assemblies other matters could also be organised. For example, the final contents of the Tenakh were determined, the pattern for regular daily prayers was established and many of the old Temple rituals were adapted for synagogue use. The supreme court of the Jewish people (the Sanhedrin) was reestablished and the head of the Sanhedrin (the Nasi) was recognised as the head of the entire Jewish community. He was entrusted with the collection of taxes, with the appointment of local judges and with the maintenance of contact between the small communities of the Jewish world. The past was not forgotten. The teachings of respected scholars such as Hillel and Shammai who had lived during the last days of the Temple were summarised. It was late in the first century CE that Rabbi Johanan ben Zakkai (a pupil of Hillel) founded the first academy. (Jews of this time were known as 'Someone son of Someone'. 'Ben' or 'bar'is the equivalent of the Welsh 'ap'.)

By the third century, these legal interpretations had become highly complex. They were preserved orally, but it was felt that the time had come to compile them into a permanent written record. There had been earlier attempts to codify (i.e. to summarise and organise) the material, but they had not been organised according to subject matter. What was needed was an authoritative record of the debates, together with the decisions of the most respected Tannaim on each particular topic. The final text was compiled by Judah ha Nasi. As his name implies, Judah was the head of the Sanhedrin and had huge prestige within the community.

The word Mishnah literally means 'passed on tradition'. The final written text was divided into six sections or orders, known as Sedarim.

The Sedarim

The first, **Zeraim** ('seeds'), deals with benedictions (blessings) and agricultural laws. The two are linked because food is a gift from God and thanking God is appropriate at the beginning of an order on agriculture. After explaining daily prayers, and the Shema and the Amidah, it explains the laws about giving food to the poor, the tithes given to the priests, the idea of the Sabbatical Year, or the seventh year in which fields must lie fallow and not be farmed. It also explains the laws about not mixing wool and linen, or sowing certain seeds together.

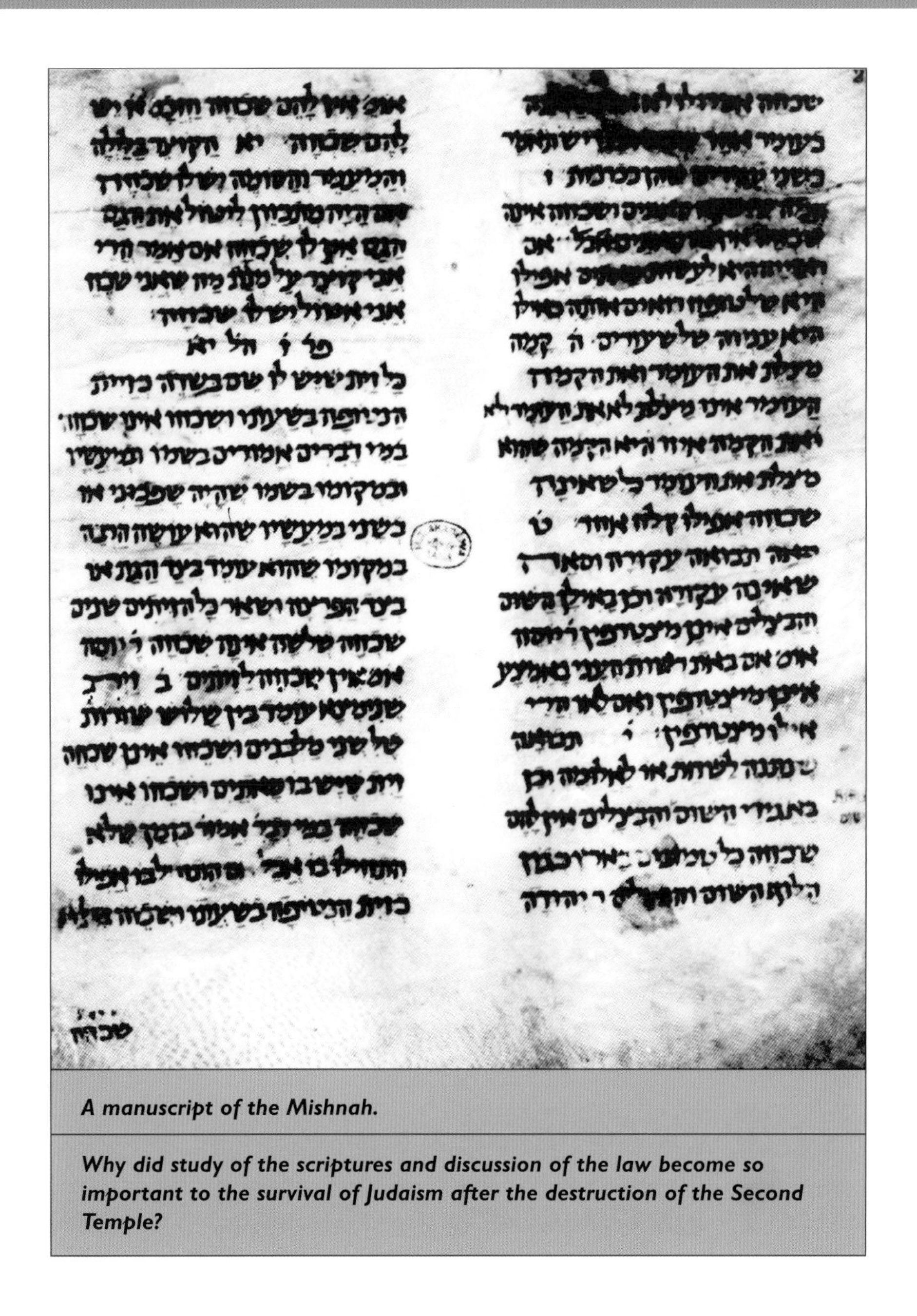

A manuscript of the Mishnah.

Why did study of the scriptures and discussion of the law become so important to the survival of Judaism after the destruction of the Second Temple?

The second, **Mo'ed** ('fixed seasons'), is concerned with the laws of the Sabbath, festival days and fast days. For example, there is much discussion on activities that are melakhot ('forbidden on the Sabbath'), and much on the obligation to remove hametz ('leaven') from the house before Pesach or Passover, as well as other technicalities regarding festival observance.

The third order, **Nashim** ('women'), mainly covers the regulation of marriage and divorce. For example it discusses the laws regarding Levirate Marriage – when a childless widow marries her deceased husband's brother so as to avoid his name dying out. It discusses a potion which should be administered to a woman who is suspected of adultery, and it also discusses the document ('get') required for divorce, issued by the husband.

The fourth, **Nezikin** ('damages'), concerns civil and criminal law including punishments and the laws of idolatry. For example it outlines administering of capital punishment, lashing, exile and so on. It discusses the laws about property, the rights of workers, buying and selling land and the swearing of oaths. In a section called avodah zarah or 'strange worship' there is a discussion of the prohibition on idolatry.

The fifth, **Kodashim** ('holy things'), discusses sacrifice and the rituals of the Temple. For example, it is in this order that kosher and pasul ('invalid') sacrifices are discussed, and in which the laws of Kashrut are to be found. There is also a description of the layout of the Second Temple in this order.

The sixth, **Tohorot** ('cleanliness'), deals with the complex subject of ritual purity. Many of the ritual purity laws became irrelevant after the destruction of the Second Temple in 70CE. However, the rules about menstruation, i.e. that a menstruating woman is impure until she has had a ritual bath ('mikveh') at the end of her period, are still observed by Jews today.

Each of the six orders contains a number of tractates (sections) and each tractate is divided into chapters. Altogether there are sixty-three tractates and five hundred and twenty-three chapters.

Sayings of the Fathers

Almost all the material is concerned with law. However there is one important exception. The ninth tractate of the order of Nezikin is known as the 'Sayings of the Fathers'. It is a delightful collection of rabbinic sayings and moral advice. It starts off establishing a chain of authority from Moses, through the elders and prophets to the 'men of the Great Assembly'. The tradition continues through Hillel and Shammai, through their pupil Rabbi Gamaliel II, through his son Simeon, through his son Judah haNasi and finally through Judah's son, a third Gamaliel. It is therefore claimed that these sayings go right back to early times.

The 'Sayings of the Fathers' is the best-known and best-loved part of the Mishnah. It is printed in most editions of the Jewish prayer book and is highly quotable: ' Upon three things is the world based: upon Torah, upon service and upon the practice of charity... Be of the disciples of Aaron, loving and pursuing peace, loving your fellow creatures and drawing them towards the Torah....If I am not for myself, who will be for me? And if I am for myself, who am I? And if not now, when?'

There is also a famous statement about loving one's neighbours:
Let not a man accustom himself to say, "Love the wise and hate the disciples, love the disciples, but hate the ignoramus, but rather, "love all", and hate only the heretics, the apostates and the informers," as David says, "Do I not hate them that hate thee?" "You shall love your neighbour as yourself, I am the Lord."

The laws of the Mishnah

The laws of the Mishnah are presented according to a set formula. Within the academies the laws of the Torah were discussed. The aim was to resolve any ambiguity so that no one could break the law in error. For example, the Book of Deuteronomy indicates that after a man has divorced his wife, he may not take her back in certain circumstances: 'Suppose a man enters into marriage with a woman, but she does not please him because he finds something objectionable about her, and so he writes her a certificate of divorce, puts it in her hand and sends her out of his house; she then leaves his house and goes off to become another man's wife. Suppose the second man dislikes her and writes her a bill of divorce and puts it in her hand and sends her out of his house, (or the second man who married her dies); her first husband who sent her away, is not permitted to take her again to be his wife...' (Deuteronomy 24: 1-3).

The question then arises, may a man ever remarry a former wife, or is she only forbidden to him if she has been with another man? This is how the Tannaim tried to resolve the problem: 'If a man divorces his wife because of her bad reputation, he may not take her back; and if, because of a vow, he may not take her back. Rabbi Judah says: if he divorces her because of a vow that many people know about, he may not take her back, but if only a few people know about it, then he may take her back. Rabbi Meir says: He may not take her back if the vow needed the opinion of a sage to revoke, but for any vow that he could revoke himself he could take her back...Rabbi Jose ben Rabbi Judah says: Once in Sidon a man said to his wife, "I will give everything away if I do not divorce you!" And he divorced her. But the sages allowed him to take her back as a precaution for the good of everyone. If a man divorces his wife because she is barren, Rabbi Judah says: He may not take her back. But the sages say: He may take her back' (Mishnah: Gittin IV).

The authority of the majority

Because the Mishnah is the record of these legal discussions, all the various opinions are included. The final and correct decision, (which was arrived at by a majority vote,) is the one that is listed last. So, in the above passage, Rabbi Judah, for all his learning and prestige, is in the wrong. The majority ('the sages') agree that a man may take his barren wife back. It did not matter how saintly or clever an individual was, the majority decision was what counted.

There is a famous story about Rabbi Eliezer. He had used all possible arguments to persuade the academy that he was in the right, even going so far as to perform a series of miracles. The sages ignored him. They said they would not pay attention even to a voice form Heaven because the Torah said 'By a majority you are to decide' (Exodus 23: 2, according to the rabbis' interpretation). The story goes on that later Rabbi Nathan met the prophet Elijah. He asked him what God did when his voice was ignored. Elijah replied that He had laughed and had said that his children had conquered Him!

The Tosefta

Parallel to the Mishnah is another collection of the oral law. This is known as the Tosefta (literally 'Supplement'). It is also divided into six orders with the same names as those of the Mishnah. No one knows the exact relationship between the two collections. It is probable that the Tosefta is merely a more extensive record of the sages' discussions. In addition, scattered through the Babylonian and Palestinian Talmuds (see Chapter 4), there are further sayings of the Tannaim which are not included in the completed Mishnah.

However, although it does not cover everything, the Mishnah is a remarkable volume. When Judah haNasi, its compiler, was dying, he is said to have asked for a peaceful resting place, since he had laboured so diligently in the study of the law during his lifetime. A voice from Heaven assured him that he would enter into peace. By codifying the whole morass of oral law and by writing it down, he had provided a solid foundation for further discussion and interpretation.

Seminar topic

Explore the advantages and disadvantages of giving the final authority in legal matters to 'the majority', rather than to learned individuals.

The Midrash

Besides developing the oral law, the Tannaim were concerned with the interpretation of the text of the Tenakh. They were convinced that the Bible was a sacred text and that it could provide both knowledge about the will of God and a guide to day-to-day living. They believed that through diligent study and by following careful rules of interpretation, God's will for his Chosen People would be revealed. Such studies, known as Midrashim, include stories, legends, parables and moral regulations all based on the Tenakh.

The rabbinic interpretation of scripture is of two kinds. The first merely involves explaining the precise meaning of a particular passage. In the second, the text is used to support a theological idea or to justify certain rules of conduct.

An example of the first kind is the Midrash on Deuteronomy 15: 11, 'You shall open wide your hand to your brother.' The Tannaim explained that this means that you should help your brother in a way that is appropriate to him: 'To him for whom bread is suitable, give bread; to him who needs dough, give dough; to him for whom money is required, give money; to him for whom it is fitting that you put bread in his mouth, put it in.'

The second type of Midrash starts from the ethical or theological point to be made and works back to the text. In writing about Deuteronomy 1: 17, ('You shall not be partial in judgement'): 'When you are judging and there comes before you two men of whom one is rich and the other poor, do not say, "The poor man's words are to be believed, but not the rich man's." But just as you listen to the words of the poor man, so listen to the words of the rich men, for it is said, "You shall not be partial in judgement.' Similarly on Exodus 34: 27, ('Write these words; in accordance with these words I have made a covenant with you'): 'When God revealed himself at Sinai to give the Torah to Israel, he gave it to Moses in order- Bible and Mishnah...'Write these words' refers to the Bible; 'in accordance with these words' applies to the Mishnah which keeps Israel separate from the heathen.'

Rules of interpretation

Even before the destruction of the Temple in 70CE, the rabbis had devised and agreed seven rules for interpreting the Tenakh. These were expanded to thirteen in the academies of the second century. One rule involved inference (working it out) from a less important to a more important case. If a law applies in a case of minor importance, then it also must apply in cases of major importance. The Sabbath is the most important of all the festivals (see Chapter 5). If an action should be avoided on an ordinary festival, it is obvious that it is even more important that it is avoided on the Sabbath.

These thirteen rules are complicated and technical and to modern readers they can seem nit-picking and over-particular. They did however ensure that there was general agreement on the ways in which the text should be explained. This was to provide the basis for a strong tradition of Jewish learning that was to ensure the survival of the whole tradition.

Tasks

Writing tasks	
	Explain and illustrate the ways in which Jews relate their daily lives to scripture.
	'Tradition is just as important as scripture in determining the daily lives of Jews'. Assess the validity of this view.

Glossary

Diaspora	Anywhere, outside of Israel, where Jews live.
Dispersion	In 70CE with the sacking of Jerusalem and the destruction of the Temple by the Romans, the Jews were 'Dispersed.'
Judah haNasi	Descendent of Hillel and complier of the Mishnah. He lived in Palestine in the 2nd Century.
Kosher	'Permitted' food which is fit for consumption according to the Jewish dietary regulations (Kashrut).
Midrash	Rabbinic interpretation of the Hebrew bible.
Mishnah	The record of the legal discussions which took place in the academies formed by the Tannaim.
Rabbinic interpretation	There is a great tradition in Judaism of discussion and scholarship of the law, both written and oral, by learned scholars and teachers known as Rabbis. The Rabbis gained a great deal of importance after the destruction of the Second Temple, when their interpretation of matters of law became very important to the Jewish community.
Tannaim	'The repeaters' a group of scholars who developed the legal tradition which was ultimately organised and written down by Judah haNasi as the Mishnah.
Temple	The First Temple, built by Solomon, was destroyed by the Babylonians. It was rebuilt after the return from the Babylonian exile, but the Second Temple was destroyed by the Romans in 70CE. The Temple had provided a focus for Jewish religion. It was believed that the presence of God occupied the Holy of Holies, the innermost sanctuary. It provided the site for continuing the Biblical tradition of making sacrifices. When it was destroyed, the heart of the Jewish religion had to be found in the scriptures, and in the teachings of the Rabbis. The ritual centre of the religion was no more.

The Talmud, Codes and Responsa

Aim

After studying this chapter you should be able to evaluate the role and importance in Judaism of the Talmuds. You should be able to demonstrate knowledge and understanding of the traditions which culminated in the Talmuds, and of the importance of the academies in Diaspora Judaism. Further elaborations on and summaries of the law, and the mechanics of Responsa are also explored, and you should be able to assess the importance of the legal tradition for different groups of Jews in the world today.

By the end of the second century CE, there were important academies in Babylon as well as in the land of Israel. Traditionally the scholars of Babylon were called Rav ('master') in contrast to those of Israel who were called Rabbi (literally 'my master'). Collectively, these successors to the Tannaim were known as the Amoraim ('spokesmen'). In all the academies, students were taught how to apply the teachings of the Mishnah to their everyday lives and there were constant communications between both centres.

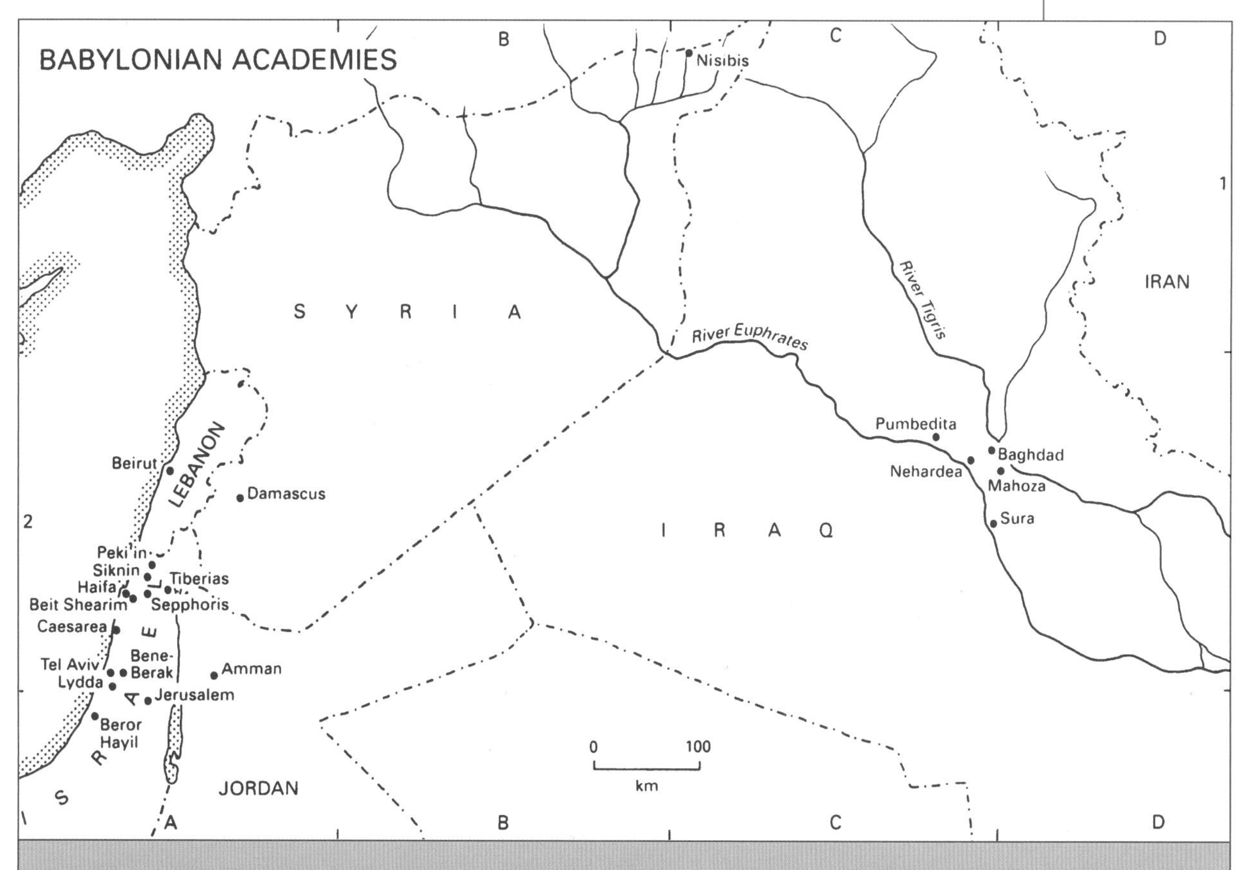

A map showing the Palestinian and Babylonian academies.

The academies became the heart of Judaism. How did they help Judaism to survive in the Diaspora?

By the end of the fourth century, the Amoraim of Palestine (which was the name the Romans had given to Israel) gathered together the teachings of the generations of rabbis since the compilation of the Mishnah. The same process occurred in Babylon in the sixth century. These volumes are known as the Palestinian (or Yerushalmi) and the Babylonian (or Bavli) Talmud. These in their turn became the foundation for further study and it eventually became necessary to compile summaries of Jewish law for everyday use. The two most famous were the Mishneh Torah of Maimonides, produced in the twelfth century and the Shulkhan Arukh of Jospeh Caro of the fifteenth century. From the early days of the academies, it also became the practice for legal authorities to publish the answers to particular legal problems. Known as responsa, these are still being issued and circulated today.

The Talmud

Like the Mishnah, both the Palestinian and the Babylonian Talmud are the record of scholarly discussions. Four of the six orders (sedarim) of Judah haNasi's Mishnah ('Seeds', 'Fixed Seasons', 'Women' and 'Damages') form the basis for further discussion and interpretation. Traditionally the Talmud is printed with the original Mishnah passage in the centre of the page with the later commentaries of the Amoraim interspersed with it. This additional material is known as Gemara ('completion'). It extends discussion of the application of the teaching of the Torah to every possible circumstance at that time. The combined text of the Mishnah and Gemara is placed in the centre of each page in the Talmud with the Tosefta and later rabbinic commentaries surrounding it. It is not known how this material was put together or whether there was ever similar material on the orders of 'Holy Things' and 'Cleanliness'. If there was, it has been lost since the Middle Ages.

The language of the Palestinian Talmud was Western Aramaic and the material came from the three important academies in Caesarea, Tiberias and Sepphoris. The Babylonian Talmud, in a slightly different Aramaic dialect, is nearly four times as long and contains about two-and-a-half-million words. It does not only contain legal material. There are legends, folklore, discussions about the nature of God, ethical teachings and magic spells. Nor is the presentation systematic: the discussion is frequently interrupted or goes off the point. The laws for copying out a Torah scroll, for example, are in the tractate concerned with cereal offerings in the Temple, and the regulations for the celebration of the festival of Hanukkah come under discussions on Shabbat.

There is a well-known Jewish legal principle that the view of a later authority is to be believed over the view of an earlier one. This means that where there are contradictions between the two Talmuds, the Babylonian version is to be preferred. Also, as time went on, the two Babylonian academies became the most important centres in the Jewish world. The academies were situated near Baghdad from where, from the seventh century on, the Caliph presided over a vast Islamic empire. Until at least the tenth century, the heads of the two academies (the Geonim) were recognised by the political authorities as being the religious heads of the Jewish community and were treated with great respect.

Task

Role play	Imagine each member of the class is one of the learned Tannaim or Amoraim. (Invent appropriate names!) Then role-play a discussion on an issue such as the food laws (kashrut) or the observance of the Passover seder, or the laws regarding marriage and divorce.

The Talmud was compiled long before the invention of printing. In order for it to be circulated in the academies, it had to be copied laboriously by hand. Inevitably errors crept in and there are many disputed variants of the text. Nonetheless, together with the Tenakh and the Mishnah, the Talmud is an authoritative text in the Jewish world. Pious Jews believe it was divinely inspired. The legal decisions of the Amoraim were thought to be as binding as those of the Tannaim. Despite internal contradictions, and despite the fact that the laws relating to the Temple sacrifices no longer apply, the whole is regarded as equally worthy of study. The principle is one of learning the law for its own sake and traditional Jewish education is centred round its study to this day.

The Codes

Because the Talmud is so diverse and about so many aspects of life, it became necessary to compile codes or summaries of the Jewish law so that ordinary Jewish people knew exactly how God expected them to behave. The earliest codes were compiled in the eighth century. They were the products of the Babylonian academies and the laws were arranged in the order of the tractates of the Talmud. Then in the late eleventh century, Isaac Alfasi, who lived in Fez in Morocco, compiled his 'Book Of Laws'. This was a summary of all the laws of the Talmud that still applied to the life of his North African community.

Maimonides and the Mishneh Torah

The most influential code of the early middle ages was that of Moses Maimonides (1135-1204). Maimonides is remembered for his contributions to both the legal and the philosophical Jewish traditions and was arguably the leading figure of mediaeval Jewry. Born in Cordoba, Spain, he and his family were compelled to flee to North Africa. His Mishneh Torah ('Second Torah') was a comprehensive summary of all Jewish law. It covered subjects that were no longer relevant, such as the ritual of the Temple, as well as the day-to-day regulations of the community. It also discussed the fundamentals of the religion including such subjects as God's nature, his qualities and the source of morality.

It is written in simple language and it is far easier to follow than the Talmud. A short extract on everyday conduct illustrates this. It is important to notice that Maimonides justified his views by quoting both the wise men (namely the Tannaim and the Amoraim) and King Solomon (in a passage from the Tenakh). Even when the law is being summarised, it must still be part of the unbroken Jewish tradition:

> 'A man should not be quick to quarrel, or envy the good fortune of others, or be lecherous or anxious for fame. The wise men say: Jealousy, ambition and lust put a man out of this world. In other words, a man should work towards the mean of each characteristic so that all his character traits are directed towards the middle path. That is what Solomon means when he says: Take heed to the path of your feet, then all your ways will be sure. Do not swerve to the right or the left.'
>
> (Proverbs 4: 26-27).

Joseph Caro: the Shulkhan Arukh and the Mappah

By the late middle ages, there were two distinct traditions among the Jewish people. The Ashkenazi tradition had its origin among Jews who lived in Northern France, Germany and Eastern Europe while the Sephardic was that practised by the Jews of Spain, North Africa and Muslim lands. Separate customs, pronunciations and prayer books developed. Communication, however, was always maintained between the two groups and the oneness of the Jewish people was never called into question.

In the fifteenthth century, Joseph Caro (1488-1575) published his hugely influential code, the Shulkhan Arukh (literally the 'laid table'). Caro was born in Spain, but he subsequently moved to Turkey and then to the land of Israel, so he was steeped in the Sephardic tradition. As a result his code was not acceptable to Ashkenazi scholars, who claimed that it ignored important French and German traditions. The problem was solved by Moses Isserles (c.1525-1572) who wrote a supplement, the Mappah (literally 'tablecloth') to incorporate Ashkenazi practices. The two volumes together became the authoritative legal code of the Jewish people.

Again, the text is straightforward and it is stressed that the law goes right back to 'Moses our teacher', and to 'the authorities':
'It is forbidden to go before a non-Jewish judge or law court for trial, even if the case would be judged in accordance with Jewish law. It is forbidden even if both parties agree to be tried before them. Anyone who is tried in a non-Jewish court is a wicked man. It is as if he has scorned, blasphemed and rejected the Law of Moses our teacher.' Moses Isserles expanded this by adding 'If a man does go before a non-Jewish court and is found guilty under their laws, but then turns round and insists that his opponent appear with him before a Jewish court, then some authorities say that he should not be heard. Others argue that he should be heard unless he has caused loss to his fellow-litigants in the non-Jewish courts. I believe it is essential to follow the former ruling.'

Caro himself was well aware of his relationship with the tradition. In another book he described how, while he was going through the Mishnah, he had a vision. A heavenly teacher promised he would be 'elevated, lifted up and made high before all the members of the heavenly academy...' because he 'busied himself all the time with the Talmud and the codes and combined the two...'

The Responsa

A responsum is an authoritative answer to a particular legal question. Letters containing responsa (plural of responsum) were sent between the academies even while the Talmud was being compiled. Later they became the major source of the continued dissemination of oral law. By the tenth century, there were communities of Jews living in all the countries around the Mediterranean Sea and throughout the Muslim empire. In order for these different communities to share in the Jewish heritage, it was necessary to keep up a regular system of contact. Letters were sent to the small, local academies (later known as yeshivot in Eastern Europe) and the replies were signed by all the senior rabbis of the institution. After a time, particularly after printing was invented, collections of these responsa were made and circulated.

Questions could be on matters of custom as well as on the law and the authorities would base their answers on the precise meaning and implication of similar concepts and situations in the Talmud. So, for example, when printing was invented, the question arose as to whether formal documents, such as marriage certificates or bills of divorce which had traditionally been written by hand could now be printed. In coming to a conclusion, the authorities examined how the terms 'write' and 'writing' were used in the sources. Only after a full review of the existing examples could they decide what was to be allowed.

Task

Class discussion	Imagine that you, as a class, are a small, isolated Jewish community in mediaeval Christian Europe, trying to practise your religion, when all those around you have different customs. Discuss the different challenges you would face, and imagine the effect of receiving a responsum from one of the Great Academies in Babylon.

Responsa for today

Even today, eminent rabbis issue responsa to particular questions. In recent years, with the development of new technology, these questions have tended to relate to completely new problems. For example, most modern refrigerators have a light which turns on automatically when the machine is opened. According to traditional teaching, it is forbidden to turn on a light on Shabbat. This is because it counts as kindling, one of the specific kinds of work forbidden by the Tannaim in the Mishnah (see Chapter 3 and Chapter 5). The question then arises whether it is permissible to open the refrigerator on the Sabbath, because it is, in effect, turning on a light.

Other interesting cases concern medical transplants. The question is: is it permissible under Jewish law to transplant the cornea from the eye of a person who has died onto the eyes of a blind person? Traditional Jewish law makes it clear that in cases of grave danger (and blindness qualifies as such) almost any measure can be taken to help a sick person. Yet the law also teaches that dead people are the source of uncleanness and all dead flesh must be buried. Some (but not all) authorities argue that an exception can be made if the dead matter is smaller than an olive. Unfortunately, the cornea is normally preserved in the eyeball and although the cornea itself is smaller than an olive, an eyeball is definitely larger. In addition, the law makes it clear that all detached limbs, such as from an amputation, must definitely be buried. Does an eyeball count as a limb?

Seminar topic

Can you think of any other issues in the modern world for which new responsa might be required?

After the Babylonian academies lost their influence in the tenth/eleventh centuries, any Jew could set himself up as a legal authority. Provided his followers accepted his wisdom, his opinions were as good as any others. This meant that the responsa did not always agree with each other. The Codes were an attempt at reconciliation, but inevitably they have given rise to further disagreement and conflicting responsa.

Yeshiva education

The Jewish people have made good use of this conflict. Even today Orthodox young men customarily finish their education at a yeshiva (academy). All activity in a yeshiva takes place in a single hall. The students study in pairs and there is a constant hubbub while together they argue out the meaning of a particular text. If they cannot agree, they leaf through all the available commentaries. Then they might consult the teacher, but even then his opinion will probably give rise to further debate. Through this process, young men hopefully develop life-long habits of independent study and coherent argument.

Seminar topic

In what situations and for what reasons might it be healthy to question the opinion of teachers?

A modern Yeshiva

Why, historically, has learning been so important in Judaism?

It must be stressed that this continued forging of the oral law is an Orthodox preoccupation (see Chapter 1). Because the non-Orthodox have abandoned the belief in the God-given authority of the Torah, they do not feel that it is necessary to keep the law in its every particular. As a result, the majority of Jews today are not interested in these legal discussions. Nonetheless, among the strictly Orthodox, the legal tradition remains of crucial importance and many families will make considerable sacrifices to ensure that their sons have a yeshiva education.

Glossary

Amoraim	Interpreters of the Mishnah who lived in Palestine and Babylonia in the 3rd-6th centuries. The Talmuds are records of their discussions
Ashkenazi Judaism	Tradition of Judaism originating in Germany and Eastern Europe, which has now spread throughout the world.
Codes	The great size and complexity of the Talmuds meant they were not accessible to ordinary people. Various scholars 'codified' (organised and summarized) them, most famously Maimonides in his Mishneh Torah.
Geonim	(singular Gaon) the honorary title given to the Head of an Academy.
Responsa	Reponses of the rabbis in the Academies of Palestine and Babylon to questions about Jewish law, which were sent to Jewish communities everywhere
Sephardi Judaism	The tradition of Judaism originating in Spain prior to the expulsion of the Jews in 1492. Sephardi Judaism has now spread all over the world.

Section 2

Aim of the section

This section will ask you to reflect on the weekly and annual festivals of Judaism, and their role in affirming Jewish identity in a changing world.

You will need to consider:

1. **The central importance of Shabbat as a sign of the Covenant, and the features of Shabbat observance.**
2. **The observance of the pilgrim festivals, the Days of Joy, Rosh Hashanah and Yom Kippur, and their affirmation of the history and values of the Jewish people.**

Jewish Life from Year to Year

The Internet

To find out more about the festivals and practices discussed in Sections 2 & 3, the Internet provides a great resource.
Have a look at **http://www.jewishfamily.com** and **http://www.zipple.com**

One of the best Jewish websites is **http://www.virtualjerusalem.com** and if you want to link up to a live 24hour a day webcam, focused on the Western Wall in Jerusalem, you'll find one on the interesting site **http://aish.com**
Notice how activity at the wall increases at Shabbat and festivals.

There is also a website for the Cardiff New Synagogue (Reform Synagogue) which includes views of the inside of the building and lists items that can be bought at the synagogue shop **http://www.cardiffnewsyn.org/**

Seminar topic

Reflect on some of the reasons why the regular observance of Shabbat and annual festivals is important to Jews.

The following four chapters describe Shabbat (the Sabbath) and Jewish festivals. Traditionally Jewish life is dominated by the regular rhythm of the weekly Sabbath and the annual festivals and fasts. Each event carries its own particular religious significance and most have their origin in God's commandments in the Hebrew Scriptures.

Festival Details		**2003**	**2004**	**2005**	**2006**
Passover *Pesach*	1st Day	Thu 17 Apr	Tue 6 Apr	Sun 24 Apr	Thu 13 Apr
	2nd Day	Fri 18 Apr	Wed 7 Apr	Mon 25 Apr	Fri 14 Apr
	3rd Day	Wed 23 Apr	Mon 12 Apr	Sat 30 Apr	Wed 19 Apr
	4th Day	Thu 24 Apr	Tue 13 Apr	Sun 1 May	Thu 20 Apr
Pentecost *Shavu'ot*	1st Day	Fri 6 Jun	Wed 26 May	Mon 13 Jun	Fri 2 Jun
	2nd Day	Sat 7 Jun	Thu 27 May	Tue 14 Jun	Sat 3 Jun
New Year *Rosh Hashanah*	1st Day	Sat 27 Sep	Thu 16 Sep	Tue 4 Oct	Sat 23 Sep
	2nd Day	Sun 28 Sep	Fri 17 Sep	Wed 5 Oct	Sun 24 Sep
Day of Atonement *Yom Kippur*		Mon 6 Oct	Sat 25 Sep	Thu 13 Oct	Mon 2 Oct
Tabernacles *Sukkot*	1st Day	Sat 11 Oct	Thu 30 Sep	Tue 18 Oct	Sat 7 Oct
	2nd Day	Sun 12 Oct	Fri 1 Oct	Wed 19 Oct	Sun 8 Oct
Shemini Atzeret *Simchat Torah*	8th Day	Sat 18 Oct	Thu 7 Oct	Tue 25 Oct	Sat 14 Oct
	9th Day	Sun 19 Oct	Fri 8 Oct	Wed 26 Oct	Sun 15 Oct

An overview of the Jewish calendar.

What are the benefits for modern Jews of annually remembering events in Jewish history? Are there any disadvantages to this practice?

The Jewish calendar

The Jewish calendar is based on the lunar cycle while the secular year is based on the solar pattern. This means that the festivals do not occur on the same date every year. However, the twelve Jewish months contain only 354 days, so the shortfall is made up by inserting a thirteenth month every few years. This means that the festivals do occur at roughly, though not exactly, the same time every year.

> 'If we want to make arrangements to go out at some time in the future, we would need to check out the date on the Jewish calendar to make sure that there is no Jewish Festival on that day. This is because we celebrate the Festivals in the synagogue and in our homes with our families and friends.
> The Jewish festivals move each year when you look at a calendar in Britain. The Jewish calendar is a lunar calendar (following the cycle of the moon) so the dates do not coincide with the dates on an ordinary calendar. So whereas New Year is always on 1st January in this country, we have to look up the dates of our festivals each year because it will vary from one year to the next.'
>
> Joyce, Swansea

Seminar topic

Why might the fact that festival dates are slightly moveable present problems for Jews in modern Britain?

Through the ages prayer and worship have been the means through which the Jewish people have expressed their deepest emotions. Before it was destroyed by the Romans in 70CE, the Temple in Jerusalem was the centre of Jewish life. Sacrifices were performed three times a day and pious Jews made the journey to Jerusalem three times a year on the pilgrim festivals of Passover (Pesach), Weeks (Shavu'ot) and Tabernacles (Sukkot) (see Chapter 6).

The Day of Atonement (Yom Kippur) was the most sacred day of the year and was the only time the High Priest entered the Holy of Holies, the inner sanctum of the Temple (see Chapter 8). According to the Book of Deuteronomy, sacrifices could be performed only in Jerusalem so once the Temple was destroyed, the sacrificial system disappeared. Instead prayer was offered three times a day in the local assembly house, the synagogue.

Tasks

Writing tasks	
	Explain the impact on Judaism of the destruction of the Temple in 70CE.
	Evaluate the view that it was extraordinary that Judaism survived without the Temple .

Continuity and consolation

Today there are several branches of Judaism and all have different traditions of worship. The Orthodox continue to hold three services a day in their synagogues. Only men are expected to attend on weekdays and a full service can only take place if ten adult men are present. The whole community comes on Shabbat and on festivals, but the men and women sit separately and the service is entirely in Hebrew. The more liberal branches of Judaism are known as Conservative and Reform in the United States and Reform and Liberal in Britain. In their synagogues, families sit together and much of the service is in English so everyone can follow it. The Hebrew Scriptures, particularly the Psalms, remain the basis of synagogue worship and the traditional forms of service probably go back to the 6th Century CE.

Between 132CE and 1948, Jews did not have a land of their own. This meant that they were always a foreign community in another country. Sometimes they prospered, but sometimes they have been cruelly persecuted. Always the rhythm of Jewish life, with its daily prayers, its weekly Sabbath and its yearly festivals, has provided continuity and consolation.

> 'The key to the festivals is the children.
> The Jewish festivals are a way of passing on our faith and our history to the next generation in the most attractive form. And the way you do this is through stories, light, food and nurture. So if the children know nothing else, they know that they will have latkes at Hanukkah, matzo at Pesach, cheesecake at Shavuot. The stomach, the heart and the mind - all three are stimulated in observing the festivals'
>
> Norma, Swansea

Seminar topic

Explain how the celebration of festivals and the observance of Shabbat have provided the Jewish community with 'continuity and consolation.'

Shabbat

Aim

After studying this chapter you should be able to evaluate the importance of the observance of Shabbat in Judaism. You should demonstrate knowledge and understanding of its biblical origins and of the various prohibitions and practices which observance involves.

The idea of a seven day week which includes one or two days of rest is ingrained in modern consciousness. In fact, it is not a natural arrangement. In the ancient world there were many holidays, but they occurred at unpredictable intervals. People might work for ten days without a break. Then there might be a single day's holiday followed by two days of work and then two more days of holiday. It was the Jews who gave the world the idea of a regular weekly day of rest. The word Shabbat means 'to rest' in Hebrew and the Jews celebrate it on the seventh day of the week, that is Saturday.

Biblical origins of Shabbat

The weekly Sabbath is considered to be the greatest and most important of all Jewish festivals. Among the Orthodox, only a person who strictly keeps Shabbat is acceptable. It is important to be shomer shabbos (a 'Sabbath keeper'). One of the reasons that they so strongly disapprove of the members of non-Orthodox movements is because they do not follow the Sabbath laws in the traditional manner. The Book of Exodus identifies Shabbat as a sign of the covenant between God and His chosen people: 'The Lord said to Moses, "Say to the people of Israel, "You shall keep my Sabbaths, for this is a sign between me and you throughout your generations, given in order that you may know that I, the Lord sanctify you" '(Exodus 31:12).

According to the Biblical texts, there are two reasons why Shabbat should be observed. In the Book of Genesis, it is described how God created the world in six days. 'Thus the Heavens and Earth were finished...and on the seventh day God finished His work which He had done, and He rested on the seventh day...So God blessed the seventh day and hallowed it' (Genesis 2:1-3). Then, in the Book of Deuteronomy, 'You shall remember that you were a servant in the Land of Egypt and the Lord your God brought you out thence with a mighty hand and an outstretched arm; therefore the Lord your God commanded you to keep the Sabbath day' (Deuteronomy 5:15). Thus, Jews must keep Shabbat holy firstly because the Creator himself did not work on the seventh day. Secondly, the Jews must remember that they themselves were slaves in Egypt, and in solidarity with all labourers they must take a day of rest.

One of the Ten Commandments concerns the Sabbath:- 'Remember the Sabbath day, to keep it holy. Six days you shall labour, and do all your work; but the seventh day is a Sabbath to the Lord your God; in it you shall not do any work, you, or your son, or your daughter, your manservant, or your maidservant, or your cattle, or the alien resident in your towns' (Exodus 20:8-10). Everyone is commanded to have a day of rest, not merely the householder and his family. The servants and animals are also included.

The rules of Shabbat

The rabbis always emphasised that Shabbat was not merely a time when work was forbidden. It was to be a day of light, peace and joy. It was a time to study the Torah, to worship God, to enjoy the company of friends and family and to relax. It is a positive merit for a husband to make love to his wife, and more delicious meals than usual were to be eaten. In order to avoid breaking the law and do work without realising it, the sages defined thirty-nine activities that were to be avoided. These include writing, baking, kindling a light, sewing, hammering, building, planting or reaping. In today's world this means that most projects around the house are forbidden as well as gardening and catching up on office work. The housewife must make all her preparation for meals before the Sabbath begins, since all food preparation is also prohibited. She should have a real rest from the domestic round of shopping, cooking, mending and cleaning.

Exodus 16:29 states that on Shabbat Jews should 'stay where you are: do not leave your place on the seventh day.' Two important interpretations of this commandment are made. Firstly it means that no-one should leave their immediate locality, and secondly it means that nothing can be carried around outside. In order to be able to engage in activities such as attending the synagogue, and carrying keys and prayer books, Orthodox Jewish communities create an eruv (a special area, for example, the particular town or village or region of the city) in which it is agreed that it is possible to move around, and to carry essentials for the observance of Shabbat. The eruv is surrounded by a symbolic fence, which may be made of real posts and wire. Everybody living within the eruv, in other words, everybody within the community within which it is possible to move on Shabbat, must also share a communal meal. Obviously in the modern world, observing the rules regarding the eruv can be terribly difficult. Local rabbis make particular rulings on the observance of eruv in their area.

The Book of Genesis describes how God created the universe. It took him six days and, at the end of every day's work, the writer declares, 'And God saw that it was good. And there was evening and there was morning, one day' (Genesis 1:5). Consequently Jews consider that days begin not in the morning, but at sunset. Shabbat starts when the sun has gone down on Friday night. This is when the household gathers together to begin their Sabbath worship and to share Sabbath joy.

שבת שלום

Friday, January 11 (Tevet 27), Sabbath begins in London at 3.59; Leeds 3.54; Manchester 3.59; Tyneside 3.48; Glasgow 3.54.

Friday, January 18 (Shevat 5), Sabbath begins in London at 4.10; Leeds 4.06; Manchester 4.11; Tyneside 4.00; Glasgow 4.06.

Sabbath lighting times as advertised in the Jewish Chronicle.

'Progress on eruv'

BARNET
RUTH ROTHENBERG

THE BARNET eruv may finally come into existence next year, when Transport for London grants a licence for placing poles and wire along the trunk roads involved, the A1, A41 and A406.

Earlier this month TfL, which is responsible for major roads, produced a draft licence which it is now negotiating with the United Synagogue eruv committee. In August, the London Borough of Barnet granted a licence for the minor roads involved.

"All my timetable predictions have so far proved over-optimistic," said eruv committee spokesman Edward Black. "But when the TfL licence is finally granted, we will be very close to the finishing line.

"I sincerely hope that within the first half of 2002, this facility will be complete," Mr Black declared.

Consider the problems faced by Orthodox Jews in fully observing Shabbat in non-Jewish areas.

Seminar topic

Consider the question of whether such a day of rest is both desirable and possible in the modern world.

Keeping Shabbat: Friday evening

Shabbat begins with the mother of the household lighting Sabbath candles. Kindling a light is one of the activities which is forbidden on the Sabbath, so this must be done before sunset. As the flame takes hold, she recites the benediction, "Blessed art thou, O Lord our God, King of the Universe, who has sanctified us by His commandments and hast commanded us to kindle the Sabbath lights."

Lighting the Sabbath candles.

Would modern society benefit from rituals which 'set apart' particular times of the week for rest or religious activities?

Meanwhile, in an Orthodox household, the men of the family will have walked to synagogue. There the Sabbath is welcomed. One element of the service is a famous mediaeval hymn, 'Come my friend to meet the bride. Let us welcome the presence of the Sabbath.'

On the Sabbath the men walk, rather than drive in the car. This is because driving is prohibited since it involves ignition. Because of this, Orthodox families must live within walking distance of the synagogue. Jewish people tend to settle in groups and, in cities where there are large Jewish populations, certain areas of the city become known as 'Jewish areas'.

Learning about lighting the Sabbath candles and practising the benediction.

Examples are Golders Green in London and Cyncoed in Cardiff. Non-Orthodox Jews, on the other hand, do not feel they should refrain from driving on the Sabbath. They argue that turning the ignition key of a motor car in no way constitutes work. Therefore Reform synagogues are built with large car parks because everyone drives and many people live a considerable distance away.

On returning home, the Orthodox man blesses his wife and children. Quoting from the book of Proverbs, he suggests that his wife is more precious than rubies (31:10-12) and he prays that his children should be like the faithful Jews of old. The boys should be like Ephraim and Manasseh (sons of the patriarch Joseph) and the girls like Sarah, Rebekah, Leah and Rachel (the matriarchs of the Book of Genesis).

Task

Research task	Discover, from the Torah, the qualities exhibited by Ephraim, Manasseh, Sarah, Rebekah, Leah and Rachel.

The family meal

The Sabbath table is laid with the best china and glass. The father says Kiddush (a prayer of sanctification) over a glass of wine and everyone takes a sip. Then the father ritually washes his hands and says a blessing over the Sabbath bread. Normally there are two plaited loaves (known as challah) symbolising the two portions of manna that the Israelites received in the wilderness every Friday (see Exodus 16:22-26). After the benediction, ('Blessed art Thou, O Lord our God, King of the Universe, who bringest forth bread from the earth'), the bread is broken and shared around.

The Friday night meal is the central family occasion of the week. It is strongly felt within the community that no Jew should be without a place to go on Shabbat, so frequently there are guests at the table. It is a chance to catch up on family news, a time to sing traditional Sabbath songs and, in Orthodox households, it is customary to discuss some element of Jewish law and practice. Jews are generally admired for their strong family life and the regular Friday night dinner at home is an important element in maintaining it.

Seminar topic

Explain why observing Shabbat is seen as contributing to the strength of family life.

The food should be the best of the week. The stove cannot be lit, but it is permissible to keep the oven on low throughout the twenty-four hours so food that is already prepared can be served hot. In America and Britain, the traditional Sabbath meal is chicken soup with dumplings, followed by roast chicken with an array of vegetables, followed by some sort of fruit dessert. There can be no mixing of meat and dairy foods (see Chapter 10), but as long as the dietary laws are kept, any food can be eaten.

After the meal, a long and beautiful grace is sung. This is an ancient prayer and goes back hundreds of years. In an Orthodox household, the Sabbath candles burn themselves out while the electric lights will be on time-switches so they turn themselves off automatically. Again, this is to observe the law against kindling or extinguishing a light. Everyone knows when this will happen and will be in bed in time.

The entrance to the synagogue in Cyncoed, Cardiff.

Non-Orthodox Jews follow a modified version of the above. Any remotely observant Jewish family will light the candles, but they may not be too particular to do it before sunset. There may be a special meal that all the family are expected to attend and the blessings over the wine and bread and a version of the grace after the meal may be recited. However, time-switches for the electric light and slow-burning ovens kept alight for the whole of Shabbat will be found only among the strictly Orthodox.

Keeping Shabbat: Saturday

In an Orthodox family, everyone will walk to synagogue for the Saturday morning service. Because artificial contraception is frowned upon by the strictly Orthodox, they tend to have large families. In any 'Jewish area', family groups can be seen walking together, fathers with groups of little boys, mothers with the girls all in their Sabbath best.

In the Orthodox synagogue the men sit at the front while the women sit either in a gallery or behind a screen. This is because the sages taught that women might distract men from prayer.

Task

Class discussion	Is it a good idea to separate women from men in worship?

In the synagogue, the prescribed morning service is centred around a reading from the Torah scrolls and another reading from the prophetic literature, Neviim. The whole Torah is divided into portions so that the whole scroll can be read over the year (see the Festival of Sukkot). Each weekly portion is divided into seven parts so that seven different members of the congregation can be called up onto the central platform to recite a blessing before and after the reading. This is regarded as an important honour within the community. An eighth person is called up for the Haftarah ('prophetic reading').

The remainder of the service is not dissimilar to that of the normal daily morning service, although the introductory prayers are different. As always the Shema prayer is recited:

The Shema (Deuteronomy 6: 4-9; 11:13-21, Numbers 15: 37-41)

Hear, O Israel: the Lord your God, the Lord is One: and you shall love the Lord your God with all your heart, and with all your soul, and with all your might. And these words which I command you this day shall be upon your heart; and you shall teach them diligently to your children, and shall talk of them when you sit in your house, and when you walk by the way, and when you lie down, and when you rise. And you shall bind them as a sign upon your hand, and they shall be as frontlets between your eyes, and you shall write them on the doorposts of your house and on your gates.

And if you obey my commandments which I command you this day, to love the Lord your God and to serve him with all your heart, and with all your soul, he will give the rain for your land in its season, the early rain and the later rain, that you may gather in your grain and your wine and your oil. And he will give grass in your fields for your cattle, and you shall eat and be full. Take heed lest your heart be deceived, and you turn aside and serve other gods and worship them, and the anger of Lord be kindled against you, and he shut up the heavens so that there be no rain, and the land yield no fruit, and you perish quickly off the good land which the Lord gives you. You shall therefore lay-up these words of mine in your heart, and in your soul; and you shall bind them as a sign upon your hand, and they shall be as frontlets between your eyes. And you shall teach them to your children, talking of them when you are sitting in your house, and when you are walking by the way, and when you lie down, and when you rise. And you shall write them upon the doorposts of your house and upon your gates, that your days and the days of your children maybe multiplied in the land which the Lord swore to your fathers to give them, as long as the heavens are above the earth.

The Lord said to Moses, 'Speak to the People of Israel and bid them to make tassels on the corners of their garments throughout their generations, and put upon the tassel of each corner a cord of blue; and it shall be to you a tassel to look upon and remember all the commandments of the Lord, to do them, not to follow after your own heart and your own eyes, which you are inclined to go after wantonly. So you shall remember and do all my commandments, and be holy to your God. I am the Lord your God, who brought you out of the Land of Egypt, to be your God: I am the Lord your God.

Many of the other prayers refer to the special blessings of Shabbat. The service concludes with the Kaddish and the Alenu prayers. The Kaddish expresses a longing for universal peace and the Alenu proclaims God as king over all the world. There is also an afternoon service in the synagogue that includes a reading of the first section of the next week's Torah portion.

At home it is compulsory to eat three meals during the course of Shabbat. By modern standards this may not sound very much, but in the past, in poor communities, it was a welcome change from the monotony and scarcity of the everyday diet. In order that Shabbat should be properly celebrated, it was customary to hoard all the best food until the end of the week. By wearing special, non-working clothes, and by eating better food, the community made Sabbath a really special day.

The Havdalah

As the sun sets on Saturday evening, the end of the Sabbath is commemorated by the Havdalah ('dividing') ceremony, which generally takes place at home. The ritual consists of blessings over wine, lights and spices. First the benediction is said: 'Blessed art Thou, O Lord, who makest a distinction between the holy and the profane, between light and darkness, between Israel and the peoples, between the seventh day and the six working days. Blessed art Thou O Lord, who makest a distinction between the sacred and the everyday.'

The light is a plait of several thin white candles. The plait represents the intermingling of the holy and the worldly and lighting it shows that the Sabbath has come to an end. The flame is extinguished by plunging it into the cup of wine and the spice box is passed around so that everyone can breathe deeply from it. The origin and meaning of this custom is obscure. One explanation is that during the Sabbath the pious Jew receives an additional soul, a special Sabbath spirituality. When this leaves him at the end of the day, smelling the spices gives him a little 'lift' before he returns to the humdrum world of weekly work.

Non-Orthodox Jews may perform some of these rituals. They may go to synagogue (probably by car) for a morning service, particularly if a Bar Mitzvah boy or Bat Mitzvah girl is reading from the Torah scroll (see Chapter 9). They may try to spend time with the family and they may even perform the havdalah ritual. But, in general, they do not observe (follow) the details of the traditional law.

It is among the strictly Orthodox that the old ways survive and the true Sabbath spirit prevails. They dress in their best; they share the three Sabbath meals; they walk to and from the synagogue together and they have the leisure to enjoy each other's company. Among them, there is a mood of extraordinary tranquillity, family solidarity and real Sabbath joy.

Nice spice

A NEW monthly series of havdalah services especially for children will be beginning this month at Northwood Synagogue, in Murray Road, Northwood, Middlesex.

The first service takes place during Chanucah, at 5.15pm on Saturday, December 15, and there will be latkes and doughnuts for all, plus a story from the synagogue's minister, Rabbi

The "Spice Girls and Boys" services will take place once a month throughout the winter, and all are welcome.

If you want to find out more information, you can contact the synagogue office on

Consider the difficulties of encouraging young Jews to observe customs that are centuries old.

Glossary

Alenu	(Aleinu le shabbe'ah) 'It is our duty to praise'. The closing prayer of the Jewish prayer book, and of services.
eruv	'mixture' (i.e. of public and private) an area within which it is possible to transport items not associated with work on Shabbat.
Havdalah	'dividing', 'separation' the ceremony at the end of Shabbat which marks the end of the holy time and the beginning of the ordinary working week.
Kaddish	A hymn of praise recited at the end of sections of liturgy, used every Sabbath.
Kiddush	Blessing said over the wine at Shabbat.
Shabbat	Sabbath, sunset Friday to sunset Saturday. The seventh day of the week during which a great number of mitzvot must be kept, and all should abstain from work.
Shema	The declaration of God's oneness, which is recited during services, and traditionally recited twice daily.

Pilgrim festivals

Aim

After studying this chapter you should be able to evaluate the role and importance in Judaism of the observance of the Pilgrim Festivals of Pesach, Shavu'ot and Sukkot. You should be able to demonstrate clear knowledge and understanding of the practices associated with these festivals, their key themes and the symbolism of items and activities. You should also be able to show the ways in which observance of them contributes to Jewish identity.

The Pilgrim festivals are so called because, according to the Book of Deuteronomy, the Jewish people are to make pilgrimage three times each year: 'Three times a year all your males shall appear before the Lord your God at the place which He will choose; at the Feast of Unleavened Bread (Pesach), at the Feast of Weeks (Shavu'ot) and at the Feast of Booths (Sukkot). They shall not appear before the Lord empty-handed" (Deuteronomy 16:16). We know from the New Testament (for example the story of the coming of the Holy Spirit in the Acts of the Apostles (Chapter 2)) that in the days of the Temple, huge numbers went to Jerusalem to offer sacrifices.

Pesach

All the pilgrim festivals are connected with the agricultural year as well as with important events in the history of the Jewish people. Pesach celebrates the beginning of the barley harvest and is a spring festival. It occurs in the month of Nisan and lasts seven nights and days in the land of Israel and eight elsewhere.

Harry & Jack with their grandfather in Swansea, saying the blessing and breaking the Matzot (unleavened bread which is eaten during Passover).

The Book of Exodus teaches that when the Jews were slaves in Egypt, God sent ten plagues to force the King to allow them to flee the country. The whole story can be found in the Book of Exodus (Chapters 5-12). The final plague was the death of the first-born. All the eldest children in every family and every first-born animal suddenly died. Only the Jewish children were spared. They had been told that each family should slaughter a lamb and should smear its blood on the doorposts of their houses. When the Angel of Death saw the blood, he 'passed over' that household. Before 70CE, before the Temple was destroyed, lambs were sacrificed on the first day of the festival and they were roasted and eaten with bitter herbs.

Pesach is also called the Festival of Unleavened Bread. After this terrible tenth plague, the King of Egypt did give the Jews permission to leave. They were in such a hurry to go that they baked their bread without giving it time to rise. To this day, Jews eat no leavened goods during Passover and, instead of bread, they eat a type of biscuit known as matzot (for the food laws of Passover, see Chapter 10).

The Passover story represented in a painting by Arthur Szyk.

The Passover seder

The main focus of the festival is the Passover meal, known as the seder. This takes place on the first and (outside Israel) also on the second night. The meal is designed to obey the commandment in the Book of Exodus, 'And you shall tell your son on that day, it is because of what the Lord did for me when I went out of Egypt' (Exodus 13: 8).

The table is laid with a group of symbolic foods in the centre. There are bitter herbs (generally horseradish) representing the bitterness of slavery. Green herbs (probably parsley) show that this is a spring festival. Salt water reminds the diners of the tears shed by the enslaved Jews. Three pieces of matzot are reminiscent of the double portion of manna found on Shabbat and festivals during the Jews' wanderings before they reached the Promised Land. The middle piece is described as 'the bread of affliction' during the course of the service. There is also haroset (a mixture of apples, nuts, cinnamon and wine) which symbolises the mortar that the enslaved Jews had to mix in Egypt. Finally, an egg and a lamb bone commemorate the seasonal sacrifices in the Temple.

According to tradition, the Messiah, God's chosen king, will reveal himself during the season of Pesach and the prophet Malachi predicted that the Messiah would be heralded by the Prophet Elijah (Malachi 4: 5). On the table, a cup is laid for Elijah and, during the course of the service, the front door of the house is opened in the hope that this year will be the year and Elijah will be waiting outside. Everyone present drinks four cups of wine. These are linked with the four expressions of redemption in the Book of Exodus: 'I will bring you out...I will deliver you...I will redeem you...and I will take you for My people' (Exodus 6: 6-7).

The symbolic food is eaten during the course of the meal. Blessings are said, songs are sung and the Passover story is told. After the meal the service ends with the long-cherished hope, 'Next Year in Jerusalem!' For nearly two thousand years, between 70 and 1948CE, it seemed highly unlikely that the Jews would ever return to the land of Israel, but every year the hope was kept alive during the Passover celebration.

> 'Jewish people are always travelling in the hope of Next Year in Jerusalem and even if you're in Jerusalem already you still say it.'
>
> Norma, Swansea

Even unobservant Jews often attend a Passover seder. It is the one occasion in the year when the whole family tries to be together and round the table there will be several generations - grandparents, aunts and uncles, cousins, parents and children, as well as several visitors. Most Jewish people have vivid memories of childhood Passovers and there is no doubt that the festival is one of the most poignant occasions of the Jewish year.

Seminar topic

Identify the main spiritual themes of the celebration of Pesach and comment on how they are relevant for Jews today.

Shavu'ot

In the days of the Temple, the barley harvest was offered on the second day of Pesach. The barley sheaf was known as the omer and the Law commanded that the Jews should count seven weeks (forty-nine days) from Pesach until Shavu'ot. This was known as 'counting the omer'. These days are regarded as a time of mourning. No one knows why, but traditionally no marriages should be celebrated and it is forbidden to have a haircut. There is just one day when these rules are suspended (see Lag ba-Omer in Chapter 7). According to the Book of Leviticus, 'And from the day after the Sabbath, from the day on which you bring the sheaf of the elevation offering, you shall count off seven weeks; they shall be complete. You shall count until the day after the seventh Sabbath.... On that same day you shall make proclamation, you shall hold a holy convocation (Leviticus 23: 15,21).

This 'holy convocation' is known as Shavu'ot. It is also called Pentecost, from the Greek word for fifty. In Leviticus, the Jewish people are commanded to 'present a cereal offering of new grain to the Lord. You shall bring from your dwellings two loaves of bread to be waved and made of two lengths of an ephah. They shall be made with leaven, a first-fruit to the Lord' (Leviticus 23: 17).

As with the other pilgrim festivals, Shavu'ot also commemorates an important event in Jewish history. In the Prayer Book, the festival is described as the season 'of the giving of our Torah'. The Jews, who were fleeing from the Land of Egypt, were said to have arrived at Mount Sinai in the third month, the month in which Shavu'ot is celebrated. As a result, the festival became a commemoration of the giving of the Law, the Torah, to Moses. The whole story can be found in the Book of Exodus, Chapters 19 and 20.

The customs of Shavu'ot

Thus Shavu'ot is the culmination of the harvest season which began at Pesach. It is also the climax of the Exodus story that God began with the slaughter of the first-born and the 'passing over' of the houses of the Jews. Different communities celebrate in different ways. In some places it is customary among the strictly Orthodox to stay awake all night during the festival while prayers from the Psalms and the Talmud are read in the synagogue. During the formal services, the readings include the Ten Commandments (Exodus 20) and the Book of Ruth. This is because Ruth (the ancestress of King David) was a convert to Judaism and so voluntarily took on all the laws of the Torah.

It is usual to eat dairy products during the festival. No one knows the origin of this custom; perhaps the most convincing explanation is that the Law is like milk, it nourishes and sustains the Jewish community. The synagogue is decorated with fruit and flowers. This is a reminder of the agricultural origins of the festival, but it also symbolises the beauty and the fragrance of the Torah. The festival lasts only one day in the land of Israel (two elsewhere) and it is always a time of merriment and rejoicing.

Because the giving of the Torah is being commemorated, the festival is also associated with education. It is usual to begin a child's religious education at this time of year and the first lesson is generally accompanied with some sweets - this is so that Torah study should always be associated with joy and sweetness. It is also the time that religion school classes graduate. In particular, the non-Orthodox movements have introduced the service of Confirmation. This is a ceremony for sixteen-year-olds and is designed to encourage young people to continue their religious education after their Bar or Bat Mitzvah (see Chapter 9). On Shavu'ot the entire graduating class takes the service in the synagogue to mark their new religious maturity.

Tasks

Writing tasks	Explain the ways in which Shavu'ot customs help Jews to celebrate the giving of the Torah on Mt Sinai.
	'Rituals and customs easily become mere empty habits and soon lose their meaning.' Evaluate this view.

Sukkot

Like Pesach and Shavu'ot, Sukkot has its origins in the Hebrew Scriptures: 'On the fifteenth day of the seventh month and for seven days is the feast of booths (tabernacles). On the first day shall be a holy convocation; you shall do no laborious work. Seven days you shall present offerings by fire to the Lord; on the eighth day you shall hold a holy convocation and present an offering by fire to the Lord; it is a solemn assembly' (Leviticus 23:33-36) The text goes on: 'You shall take on the first day the fruit of goodly trees, branches of palm trees and boughs of leafy trees and willows of the brook; and you shall rejoice before the Lord your God for seven days...You shall live in booths for seven days...that your generation may know that I made the Children of Israel dwell in booths when I brought them up out of the Land of Egypt' (Leviticus 23: 40, 42, 43.)

'Sukkot - I loved it. Good memories. I remember being in the cheder (Jewish class) with Dad, and the cheder children putting the sukkah together, and I used to love the smell of the fruit.'

Dani, Swansea

A sukkah built by the children of Caio Primary School, Carmarthenshire.

Sukkot, then, reminds the Jewish people of their time of wandering in the wilderness before they reached the Promised Land of Israel. The story can be found in the Book of Exodus 16 and 17. To fulfil the commandment, they must construct a booth or tabernacle (sukkah) and main meals should be eaten in it for the duration of the festival. In a cold climate, such as Wales, there is no obligation to sleep in it or to remain in it if it rains.

'I used to go with my father in his van, driving up on to the mountain and cutting the ferns that grew everywhere. We would then take them back home to make the covering for the sukkah. We had some old doors in the garage which we would use each year to make the sukkah, binding them together, and then when Sukkot was over, we took them down and stored them for the following year. We used to eat our food in there as long as it wasn't raining.'

Alan, Swansea

The sukkah and the lulav

The sages of the Talmud explain precisely how the sukkah should be built. It has to be at least four cubits square (approximately two meters). It should have at least three walls and the roof covering should be made of things that were once growing. In fact the roof should not be very substantial. When the pious Jew stands in his tabernacle, he should be able to see the stars. Traditionally the structure is decorated with flowers and fruit because tabernacles is also a harvest festival and occurs in September.

> 'Sukkot was always fun. We were collected from the cheder, and we used to help tie up all the fruit in pieces of net and hang them from the roof which was open so you could see the sky - and we wouldn't have to study in the cheder that day.'
>
> Lisa, Swansea

In order to obey the commandment of taking 'the fruit...the branches...the boughs and the willows', a bundle known as the lulav is made. This is composed of palm, willow and myrtle and a citron fruit is held in the other hand. During the festival services in the synagogue, the lulav is waved to the north, the south, the east, the west, upwards and downwards. This probably symbolises God's control of all the points of space. Then there is a procession around the building while Psalms 113-118 are recited and a prayer is said for a good harvest. Some authorities argue that the composition of the lulav symbolises the Jewish people. Many different types make up the whole religious community, but they must all work together in harmony.

Completing the cycle

On the seventh day, seven circuits of the synagogue are made and, for many people, this is the culmination of the whole season of penitence (the New Year, the Ten Days of Penitence and the Day of Atonement), (see Chapter 8). The next day, described in Leviticus as the day of a 'holy convocation', is known as Shemini Atzeret (the 'eighth day of assembly') and Simchat Torah (the 'Rejoicing of the Law'). In the Land of Israel, both are celebrated on the same day, but outside Israel the whole festival lasts an extra day and Simchat Torah is kept on the ninth day.

As on the Sabbath and on the first day of the festival, no work is permitted. The Shemini Atzeret service includes a prayer for rain during the synagogue service. The Rejoicing of the Law is a very joyful occasion. This is when the annual reading of the Torah is completed and the cycle begins again with the first portion from the Book of Genesis. It is regarded as an honour to be called up for the final reading from the Book of Deuteronomy and the man chosen is known as the 'Bridegroom of the Law.' The man who reads from Genesis is the 'Bridegroom of Genesis'. The Scrolls of the Law are taken out during the course of the service and are carried in procession around the synagogue with much rejoicing. Among the strictly Orthodox, this is a tremendous celebration and the procession may spill out of the synagogue building into the neighbouring streets. Often a splendid party is given by the 'two bridegrooms'. For the

Orthodox who live every detail of their lives in accordance with the commands of the Law, nothing can be too good to express joy and gratitude to God for his gift of the Torah.

Glossary

Convocation	Assembly – a meeting together.
Pesach	Or Passover. Also known as the Feast of the Unleavened Bread, which remembers the liberation of the Israelites from Egypt under the leadership of Moses.
Pilgrim festivals	In the days of the Temple, those festivals during which people would go there to make sacrifices. The three Pilgrim festivals are Pesach, Shavu'ot and Sukkot.
Shavu'ot	The Feast of weeks, which celebrates the giving of the Torah to Moses.
Sukkot	The Festival of Booths, the autumn festival during which a tent (Sukkah) is erected to remember the wandering of the Israelites in the desert.
Omer	The period between Pesach and Shavu'ot.
Seder	'Order', the order of service in Jewish ritual. Seder refers particularly to the ritual of the Passover meal.
Simchat Torah	The last day of the festival of Sukkot, when the cycle of Torah readings comes to an end, and starts again at the beginning of Genesis.

Days of Joy

Aim

After studying this chapter you should be able to evaluate the role and importance in Judaism of the observance of the Days of Joy. You should be able to demonstrate clear knowledge and understanding of the practices associated with these festivals, their key themes and the symbolism of items and activities. You should also be able to show the ways in which observance of them contributes to Jewish identity.

Shabbat is the most important of all the Jewish festivals. The three pilgrim feasts (Pesach, Shavu'ot, Sukkot), like Shabbat have their origin in the Torah and are celebrated by all religious Jews. The Days of Joy are of less significance. Only Purim has its origin in the Hebrew Scriptures. The story commemorated at Hanukkah is based on the Book of Maccabees in the Apocrypha, and the New Year for Trees, Israel Independence Day and the Thirty-third Day of the Omer all originate from later periods in Jewish history.

Purim

The feast of Esther is known as Purim in Hebrew. Purim literally means 'lots' and is a reference to the casting of lots to determine the day for the destruction of the Jews. According to the story, Haman, the chief minister of King Ahasuerus of Persia, was determined to destroy all the Jews in the kingdom. His wicked plans were foiled through the intervention of the virtuous Mordecai, whose niece was Ahasuerus's queen. She pleaded for her people and the tale ends with Haman being hanged to universal rejoicing on the gallows prepared for Mordecai.

Traditionally, on the day before the festival, a fast is held. This is because Queen Esther proclaimed a fast before she spoke with her husband. The next day is one of celebration and, according to the biblical Book of Esther, the feast was instituted by Mordecai himself: 'And Mordecai recorded these things and sent letters to all the Jews....enjoining them that they should keep the fourteenth day of the month of Adar and also the fifteenth day of the same, year by year, as the days on which the Jews got relief from their enemies, and as the month that had been turned for them from sorrow into gladness...days of feasting and gladness, days for sending choice portions to one another and gifts to the poor' (Book of Esther, 9: 20-22).

Normally celebrations take place in the synagogue. During the service, the Book of Esther is chanted to a traditional melody. There is a carnival atmosphere and the children attend in fancy dress, often as Esther or Mordecai.

During the course of the reading, whenever Haman's name is mentioned, there is an attempt to drown it with foot-stamping and noise-makers. Little sketches are put on and traditionally this is the one occasion in the year when students are permitted to imitate the idiosyncrasies of their teachers.

After the reading there is a special prayer of thanksgiving for Jewish deliverance and everyone shares in a special festival meal. This tends to be much like a children's party; a special kind of cake is baked, known as Hamantashen ('Haman's hats'), which are small pastry triangles filled with dried fruit or poppyseed. According to the sages, so much wine should be drunk that the participators should no longer be able to distinguish between Haman and Mordecai! Parents give their children small gifts of money and parcels are sent to the poor.

Modern day Purim

A Purim parade.

Explain the relevance for modern Jews of dressing up and acting out the Purim story.

Purim is traditionally regarded as a minor festival. At the end of the nineteenth century, among non-Orthodox Jews, there was an attempt to dismiss it as an old-fashioned folk relic. It was regarded as being too nationalistic and vindictive and its values were not to be encouraged. However, in recent years, it has assumed a new significance. After the Nazi holocaust when six million Jews were murdered, the story of the deliverance of the Jews in Persia means a great deal. Since 1948 there has been a Jewish political state. The Jews are no longer merely a religious and ethnic community. In Israel, the feast has become a time for carnival. Revellers dress in special Purim costumes and parades are held through the streets of all the big cities.

Task

Role play	Imagine you are a survivor of the Holocaust celebrating Purim in Israel. What thoughts and emotions do you experience?

Although today many Jews regard themselves as non-religious, many still want their children to know something about their heritage. It is very common for people to become members of a synagogue only because they want their children to go the religion school. Purim is traditionally a children's festival and every religion school makes a great deal of Purim games and celebrations. As a result, Jewish parents who rarely attend synagogue will go at Purim because they have become involved, either making costumes, or baking for the party, or because they want to see their children perform.

Some Jewish communities also celebrate other Purims, remembering particular times in their own history when they were delivered from danger. On all these occasions, the message is the same: even when surrounded by peril, God has not forgotten the Jews. God is at work and always, in his own way, he is striving to preserve his people.

Hanukkah

The Hebrew word for the festival of Lights is Hanukkah and it is celebrated for eight days. The story goes back to the second century BCE. At that time the Land of Israel was being ruled by a series of Hellenistic (Greek) kings who wished the people to convert to Greek religion. To this end they desecrated the Temple in Jerusalem and they tried to ban the practice of the Jewish religion. However they were overcome by the Maccabee family who led a rebellion. After a three-year struggle, Jerusalem was recaptured and the Temple was rededicated. According to a talmudic legend, only a very small quantity of sacred oil could be found to light the seven-branched golden candelabrum. Amazingly, the supply lasted for eight full days, which gave the religious authorities time to dedicate more.

'SPURS, ARSENAL & CHELSEA ALL ABOVE MAN. UNTD. – NOW, THAT'S WHAT I CALL A MIRACLE!'

Cartoon from the Jewish Chronicle.

The majority of British Jews live in London.

The seven-branch candelabrum (Menorah) is an important and ancient symbol of Judaism. According to the Book of Exodus, when the Jews had escaped from Egypt and were wandering in the wilderness, they were instructed to build a portable sanctuary. Among the religious objects used to furnish it was a lampstand: 'You shall command the people of Israel that they bring to you beaten olive oil for the light that a lamp may be set up to burn continually' (Exodus 27:20). Thus re-lighting the candelabrum was an act of victory and, even today, the seven-branch candlestick is a symbol of the enduring dedication of the Jewish people. One is set up outside the Knesset ('Parliament') building in Israel.

Kindling the Hanukkah lights.

Why is the symbolism of light so powerful?

The customs of Hanukkah

Hanukkah is normally celebrated at home. Every observant Jewish household has a Hanukkah menorah or Hanukkiyah. This is an oil lamp or a candlestick with places for nine lights. One light is a serving-light, which is used to kindle the other flames. On the first night, the serving-light ignites one candle; on the second night two and so on. On the eighth night, the last one of the festival, all eight lights are lit and the candlestick is ablaze. Normally the candles are lit from right to left. Traditionally the candlestick should be put in a prominent place, perhaps even by a window, so that it can be seen by passers-by. They are then reminded of the faithfulness of God to his people.

Various games are associated with the festival, the best-known of which involves a spinning top or dreidl. This is inscribed with four Hebrew letters that form an acrostic for the Hebrew phrase, 'a great miracle has occurred here' and there are rules for spinning the dreidl. It is quite possible to make both the dreidl and the Hanukkah menorah at home and this is an opportunity for family creativity.

It is also customary to eat potato pancakes, sugar doughnuts and nuts after the menorah has been lit (although this varies with different communities). Even at home the hymn 'Maoz Tsur' ('Rock of Ages'), which goes back to the thirteenth century, or Psalm 30 is sung.

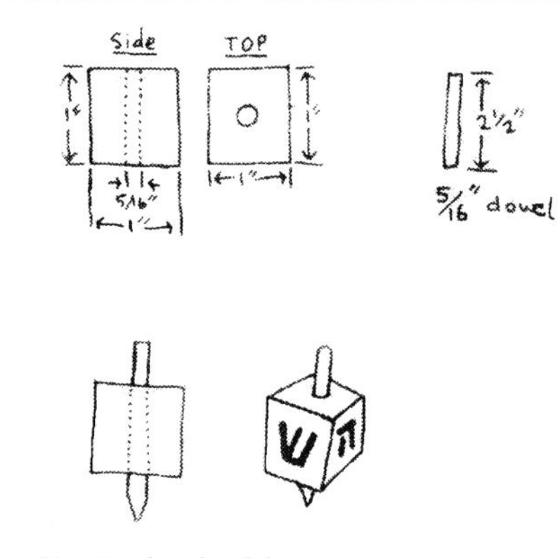

How to play dreidel

Everyone in the game starts with 10 or 15 pennies (nuts, raisins, matchsticks, etc.) Each player put one of these in the middle (called The Pot). The driedel is spun by one player at a time. Whether he wins or loses depends on which face of the driedel is up when it falls.

Num means nisht or "nothing". Player does nothing.
Gimmel means gantz or "all". Player takes everything in The Pot.
Heh, means halb or "half". Player takes half or what is in The Pot.
Shin means shtel or "put in". Player adds two objects to The Pot.

When only one object or none is left in The Pot every player adds one. When an odd number of objects are in The Pot, the player rolling heh, "half", takes the total plus one.

When one person has won everything the game is over.

A note about driedel: Apart from the fun-and-games aspect, what could be better than a spinning top to suggest the shifting of the sun, the succession of the seasons, and the spinning (and wobbling) of the earth on its axis?

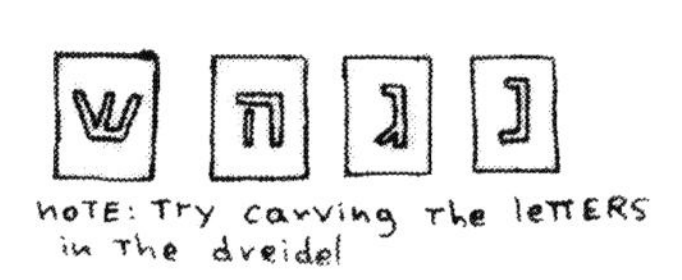

How to play dreidl.

Consider some of the reasons why small Jewish children in Britain may muddle up Hanukkah with Advent and Christmas like this.

'The children of the Cheder used to have a Hanukkah party every year, and all the children had a chance to do a turn - to sing, dance or recite - if we wanted to. The minister's wife was an accomplished pianist and she would accompany us all on the piano. She would go around the children asking them what they wanted her to play. When it came to one little girl's turn, she said she wanted to sing 'Away in the Manger'. Without hesitation, the minister's wife played it beautifully for her and the youngster sang along happily. It's typical of the Jewish way of life - to live and let live.'

Norma, Swansea

During the regular daily services in an Orthodox synagogue, the festival is commemorated with the recital of Psalms 113-118 and with the saying of various special prayers. However, traditionally, Hanukkah is regarded as a minor festival. Unlike the Pilgrim festivals, there is no command for a solemn assembly and there is no need to abstain from work.

In the last century, the festival has taken on enormous importance. The biggest Jewish community in the world lives in the United States of America. After attending a Passover seder (see Chapter 6), lighting the Hanukkah menorah has become the most observed Jewish ritual among American Jews. This is because the festival occurs around Christmas time. In recent years, the festival of Lights is generally understood as the 'Jewish Christmas' and it is not uncommon to see both a Christmas tree and a Hanukkah menorah being lit in suburban shopping centres and civic squares.

'I love Hanukkah, especially when all the family sings the Hanukkah songs together. When we were children we each had a present every night of Hanukkah after lighting the candles. We never had big presents for Hanukkah, just tiny ones like socks, pencils and toiletries - but we used to appreciate them more. You always appreciate the little things more.'

Dani, Swansea

Home celebrations are not dissimilar. Children are given presents, often one for each day of the feast. There are family gatherings, special meals and the house may be decorated. Even the symbolism is similar. Christmas celebrates the birth of Jesus, the light of the world. Hanukkah celebrates the renewal of the light of Torah in the face of difficulty and opposition. However the importance of the festival in the community does indicate the desire, even among non-religious Jews, to set themselves apart from the majority religion and to preserve their own customs.

Task

Role play	Role play a dialogue between a young American Jew and a young American Christian during which they explain Hannukah and Christmas to each other

Fun time with trees

TU BISHVAT, the Jewish New Year for trees, is just over three weeks away. At cheder or in school, you may be preparing for the festival by learning about different trees and their fruits. Perhaps you will help in planting a new tree especially for Tu Bishvat.

Edgware Synagogue is organising a "Tu Bishvat Funday" for young families in the community.

Attractions will include a bouncy castle, a ball pond, as well as tree-decorating and planting and a delicious fruit bar.

Children between the ages of three and eight — and their parents — are welcome. The Funday will take place on Sunday, January 20 between 3pm and 5pm. Admission price is £2 per child; adults are free.

If you would like more information, you can contact Rabbi [illegible] on [illegible]

This advertisement for Tu Bishvat activities shows how the festival was celebrated in a London synagogue in 2002.

The New Year for Trees

The New Year for Trees, Tu Bishvat, occurs about a month before Purim. The festival goes back to the days of the Temple in Jerusalem. In order to support the Temple, regular tithes (taxes) had to be paid. These took the form of fruit, which was laid aside throughout the year by landowners. In the Land of Israel the festival takes place at the end of the rainy season, when the new sap begins to rise in the trees and it marked the beginning of each tithe-year. In Britain the new financial year does not begin on January 1st, similarly in ancient Israel, the tithe year began on a different date from the religious New Year (see Chapter 8).

Once the Temple was destroyed in 70 CE, the system of paying tithes came to an end. Nonetheless the festival has survived. It used to be the custom to eat fifteen different types of fruit, (the festival occurs on the fifteenth day of the month of Shevat). Today, in the State of Israel, it is a very happy occasion. Children have the day off school and they all go out into the countryside. There they plant saplings to improve and conserve the land. In doing so, they are fulfilling the mitzvah (commandment) in the Book of Leviticus, 'When you come to the land, you shall plant all kinds of trees' (Leviticus 19: 23).

Israel Independence Day

Israel Independence Day is a modern festival. From the time of the destruction of the Temple in 70CE, the Jewish people prayed to return to the land promised by God in the Hebrew Scriptures. At the end of the nineteenth century, groups of pioneers began to settle in the land; they bought farms and established agricultural colonies. This movement, to establish a Jewish homeland in the Promised Land, was known as Zionism. Eventually, after six million European Jews had been murdered by the Nazis during the Second World War, the United Nations considered the possibility of establishing a Jewish State. On the 14th May 1948, the newly-elected Prime Minister read the Jewish Declaration of Independence: 'We hereby proclaim the establishment of the Jewish State in Palestine, to be called Israel.'

That was not the end of the story. Immediately the new country was attacked by the surrounding nations who felt that the land had been stolen from them. However the Israeli forces pushed them back and in 1949, the new state was recognised as an independent state within the United Nations.

Since 1948, Independence Day has been celebrated. The equivalent to 14th May in the Jewish calendar is the fifth day of the month of Iyar. Special prayers are said in the daily service in the synagogue and various official celebrations are held. Outside Israel, in places where there are large Jewish populations such as New York City, the day is also recognised with parties and parades. It is an opportunity for Jews everywhere to show their support for their co-religionists (other Jews) and for the Jewish state.

The thirty-third day of Omer

The thirty-third day of Omer is known as Lag ba-Omer in Hebrew. The season of counting the Omer, (the days between Pesach and Shavu'ot), is generally considered to be a time of mourning. No one knows precisely why this is, although various explanations have been given. In the second century CE there was a devastating plague and many eminent scholars were infected. Also during the time of the Crusades in the Middle Ages, when the Christian kings were trying to drive the Muslims from the Holy Land, many Jews were massacred. Traditionally no weddings may be celebrated, nor should anyone have their hair cut during this time.

The thirty-third day is the great exception. It occurs in the early summer and is said to be the day on which the plague stopped. It is known as the scholars' feast and it is a day of rejoicing. Students in religious academies go on picnics in the countryside and in the Land of Israel, pious Jews make pilgrimage to the tomb of a second century sage, Simeon ben Yochai, in Meron. Simeon was a hero who continued to teach and study the Torah even when it was forbidden by the Romans. He lived in hiding with his sons for thirteen years until he heard of the Emperor's death. Traditionally also this is the day that small boys have their first haircut.

Tasks

Writing tasks	Explain the ways in which celebrating the Days of Joy might help to affirm the identity of Jews living both inside and outside of Israel.
	Evaluate the view that celebrating Independence Day merely fuels Israeli nationalism.

Glossary

Esther	A Jewish woman married to the King of Persia, who managed to avert a persecution of the Jews. Her story is told in the book of Esther.
Haman	Haman, the prime-minister of Persia who tried to persuade the king to exterminate the Jews (Book of Esther).
Hanukkah	Festival of Lights, commemorating the cleansing and rededication of the Temple after its desecration by the Greek King Antiochus IV, recorded in the books of Maccabees in the Apocrypha.
Hanukkiyah	Eight-branched candlestick, the candles of which are lit during Hanukkah, to remember the eight days and nights which the Temple light burned, miraculously, without oil, after the Maccabee brothers had liberated Jerusalem and cleansed the Temple.
Knesset	The parliament of modern Israel.
Lag ba-Omer	The thirty-third day of Omer, during which celebrations are permitted, boys have their first haircuts and marriages can be made.
Purim	The 'Festival of Lots' which remembers the triumph of Queen Esther of Persia over Haman, as told in the book of Esther.

Rosh Hashanah and Yom Kippur

Aim

After studying this chapter you should be able to evaluate the role and importance in Judaism of the observance of the Rosh Hashanah and Yom Kippur. You should be able to demonstrate clear knowledge and understanding of the practices associated with the fast of Yom Kippur and the celebration of the New Year; their key themes; and the symbolism of items and activities. You should also be able to show the ways in which observance of them, and the theme of repentance and reconciliation, contributes to Jewish life and identity.

The Hebrew Scriptures teach that although human beings are created by God, all too often they choose evil over good. As the Book of Genesis puts it: 'The Lord saw that the wickedness of mankind was great on the earth, and that every inclination of the thoughts of their hearts was only evil continually' (Genesis 6: 5). According to the Torah, sacrifice was the means of removing the guilt of sin. Sacrifice could be offered only in the Temple in Jerusalem and, according to the Mishnah: 'The World stands on three things, on Torah, on the Temple service and on loving kindness.' However, the biblical prophets emphasised that sacrifice by itself was not enough. True repentance (being truly sorry) was also necessary, together with a determination to do better in the future. As the prophet Amos declares: 'Let justice roll down like waters and righteousness as an ever-flowing stream' (Amos 5: 24).

Once the Temple had been destroyed in 70CE, the sacrificial system came to an end and remorse and restitution was the only way to be released from the burden of sin. The rabbis of the talmudic period made many statements on the subject and the thirteenth century devotional writer, Jonah ben Abraham, suggested that the following were the factors involved in true repentance: remorse, shame, submission to God, confession, prayer, compensation of the victim, giving to charity, reflection on suitable punishment of the body through fasting and weeping.

Fasting in particular is regarded as a way of making atonement (making up) for sin and the Jewish community takes this duty seriously. Several days in the yearly calendar are set aside as fast days and even the most non-religious Jew is aware that autumn is the great season of repentance with the New Year (Rosh Hashanah), with the Ten Days of Penitence and with the Day of Atonement (Yom Kippur).

Seminar topic

Explain the connection between fasting and atonement for sin.

Would like to wish all their Jewish supporters a happy and healthy New Year.

ORIENT LINES WISHES ALL ITS PAST AND FUTURE PASSENGERS A VERY HAPPY AND HEALTHY NEW YEAR

ORIENT LINES

Michelin House, 81 Fulham Road, London SW3 6RD. Tel: 020

BARBARA ROCHE M.P.

Wishes all her constituents in Hornsey and Wood Green a happy and healthy New Year and well over the Fast.

28 Middle Lane, London N8 8PL
Tel: 020

CERRUTI 1881

Wishes all our clients a Happy & Healthy New Year

106 New Bond Street
London W1Y 9LG
Tel: 020

Shana Tova
to all our valued clients, past, present & future from Jason & Paul

Sovereign Photography

020
www.sovereignphotography.co.uk

What does this cutting from the Jewish Chronicle tell us about Jewish life in London?

Rosh Hashanah

Rosh Hashanah (literally 'the head of the year') is the name for the New Year in Hebrew. It takes place on the first of the month of Tishri in the autumn. It is an extremely important date in the Jewish year and has its origins in the Scriptures. According to the Book of Numbers: 'On the first day of the seventh month, you shall have a holy convocation; you shall do no laborious work. It is a day for you to blow the trumpets' (Numbers 29: 1). It is also described as a 'day of solemn rest' and a 'day of memorial'.

The Mishnah explains that all human beings stand before God at the New Year to face His judgement. A small number are recognised as fully righteous and another group are condemned as hopelessly wicked. The vast majority, however, are somewhere in-between.
They have ten full days to repent of their evil ways before the final yearly judgement that is sealed on the Day of Atonement. For these ten days their fate hangs in the balance. It is their last chance to put things right for the year.

In the synagogue, the reading desk and the Torah scrolls are draped in white. Often the rabbi and the cantor also wear white robes. The services last all day and people often remain in their seats throughout. The formal prayers emphasise God's kingship and his care and concern for all people. The Torah reading includes the story of Abraham's obedience, his willingness to sacrifice his son Isaac (Genesis 22) and among the prophetic passages is the saga of the birth of Samuel, who was dedicated to God even before he was born (I Samuel 1).

Repentance and reconciliation

The most memorable element is the blowing of the shofar ('ram's horn'). It is blown three times in set patterns during the services: once after the Torah reading, once during the additional service and once at the end of the day, before the final prayers. The twelfth century philosopher, Maimonides, explained that the ram's horn calls the Jewish people to repentance. It commands them to awake from their slumbers, to think about their deeds, to remember their Creator, to forsake their evil ways and to return to God. After the third sequence of blasts, the service ends with the promise that repentance, prayer and acts of charity can avert God's final condemnation.

It is considered special in Judaism to celebrate festivals in the Holy city of Jerusalem. Some festivals are traditionally known as 'pilgrim festivals', where every attempt is made to celebrate them in Jerusalem. For long periods of Jewish history it has not been possible to celebrate any festivals there at all, but since the creation of the State of Israel in 1948, such celebrations have become a real possibility.

Blowing the shofar in front of the Western Wall.

The day is celebrated at home with special food. As on Shabbat, wine is blessed and sanctified. Then bread and apples are dipped in honey and a special prayer is recited asking that the coming year may be a sweet one. On the second evening it is customary to eat some new season's fruit which has not been eaten before (such as pomegranate or pawpaw.) A blessing is said thanking God for preservation to this season. It is also customary to send cards to friends and family.

Rosh Hashanah is celebrated throughout the Jewish community. Even people who rarely go to synagogue will go twice a year to celebrate the New Year and the Day of Atonement. When a new synagogue is constructed, the building has to be organised in such a way (with moveable partitions or some other device) that a large congregation can be accommodated on these two days, without the building looking too empty at other times. The New Year is a solemn feast, but it is not technically a fast day. Rather it is a preparation for the fast. The next ten days, the Ten Days of Penitence, lead up to the most holy and solemn day of the year, the Day of Atonement. All through this period Penitential prayers, or selihot, are said.

Seminar topic

Just as is common at Easter and Christmas in the Christian calendar, many Jews attend their place of only worship at New Year and the Day of Atonement. To what extent might this be seen as hypocritical?

Real atonement is difficult to achieve. The (then) leaders of Israel and Palestine shake hands in 1993, at a time of relative peace.

On Yom Kippur, you'll know what it feels like not to eat for one day. The woman in this picture struggles for food every day. She is one of 1.2 billion people in the world who have to survive on the equivalent of less than $1 a day.

TARGET 2015

We want to help create a world where less people are hungry. And we're not alone. Target 2015 aims to halve the proportion of people in the world who live in absolute poverty by the year 2015. It represents an internationally agreed set of targets promoted in this country by the Department for International Development (DFID) and to which UKJAID is a committed partner.

At UKJAID - UK Jewish Aid & International Development - we aim to express in today's world the fundamental Jewish value of alleviating poverty. As it says in Pirkei Avot (Ethics of the Fathers), *"Treat the poor as members of your household"*. And we believe that should mean opening our doors to all in the world who are hungry.

There is real progress: more people have escaped poverty in the last 50 years than in the previous 500. Will you join us in this next task? For more information on Target 2015 and UKJAID, please send off the coupon, phone us on or email ukjaid@talk21.com. There's a world hungry to hear from you.

Yes, I want to halve world poverty by 2015. Please send me information on how I can become involved in helping UKJAID (Reg Charity 328 488) contribute to achieving Target 2015. (JC2)

Name...

Address..

.... Postcode ....

Telephone.................................... Email ....

Send to:

Why might Jews be thinking of the poor and starving at Yom Kippur?

Yom Kippur

The Day of Atonement (Yom Kippur in Hebrew) occurs on the tenth day of the Jewish month of Tishri. Like the New Year, it is prescribed in the Hebrew Scriptures: 'On the tenth day of this seventh month, you shall have a holy convocation and afflict yourselves; you shall do no work, but you shall offer a burnt offering to the Lord, a pleasing odour' (Numbers 29: 7-8). The Book of Leviticus describes the ceremonies in more detail. The High Priest must wear garments of holy linen. A bull must be sacrificed as an offering for sin. Then lots must be drawn between two goats. One must be sacrificed to God and the other, the scapegoat, should be sent out alone into the wilderness carrying the sins of the people with it (Leviticus 16). It was the one day of the year that the central shrine of the Temple was entered. Every year the High Priest would go inside all alone to pray for forgiveness for the Jewish people.

The text stresses that the day must be sacred for ever: 'And the priest who is anointed and consecrated as priest in his father's place shall make atonement...And this shall be an everlasting statute for you, that atonement may be made for the people of Israel once in the year because of all their sins' (Leviticus 16: 32, 34). Since there is no longer a Temple in Jerusalem, all the provisions for animal sacrifice are irrelevant, but the Day of Atonement is still observed; fasting has taken the place of sacrifice for restoring the relationship with God. Traditionally, however, amongst the very orthodox, Kapparot ('atonements') are made. This involves the slaughtering of a chicken to be given to the poor, or alternatively the giving of money to the poor, in return for the restoration of a right relationship with God.

Before the day itself, it is usual for people to seek reconciliation with anyone they might have offended. This is because prayer and fasting only brings atonement for sins against God. Sins against other people can be pardoned only if forgiveness has been sought from the injured person. During the day itself, everyone over Bar or Bat Mitzvah age (see Chapter 9), unless there is a clear medical reason against it, is expected to fast from nightfall until the sunset of the next day. This means not eating or drinking anything at all. The whole day is then spent in the synagogue.

Kol Nidre

There are five separate synagogue services. The evening service is known as Kol Nidre ('All vows') after its first prayer and it centres around prayers of confession. These always use the 'we' rather than the 'I' pronoun, stressing collective responsibility (for example, 'Our Father our King, we have sinned against you...') It is not unusual for the strictly Orthodox to remain in the synagogue throughout the night reciting the entire Book of Psalms. The morning service includes a reading from the Book of Numbers about sacrifice and a prophetic reading from Isaiah on the real meaning of fasting: 'Is it not to share your bread with the hungry and bring the homeless poor into your house?...then shall your light break forth like the dawn and your healing shall spring up speedily' (Isaiah 58: 7-8).

THE KOL NIDRE PRAYER

May we be absolved from all the vows and obligations we make to God in vain, from this Yom Kippur to the next – may it come to us for good; the duties and promises which we cannot keep, the commitments and undertakings which should never have been made.

We ask to be forgiven and released from our own failings. Though all the promises of our fellow men stand, may God annul the empty promises we made in our foolishness to Him alone, and shield us from their consequences.
Do not hold us to vows like these!
Do not hold us to obligations like these!
Do not hold us to such empty oaths.

(Braybrooke, M., *How to Understand Judaism*, SCM, 1995 p16)

Task

Writing task	Re-write this prayer in your own words.

The additional service describes the order of worship in the Temple and Jewish martyrs who have died for the faith are remembered. Readings from the Holocaust period are often introduced at this point. The afternoon service includes the list of forbidden marriages in the Book of Leviticus and a reading from the Book of Jonah that emphasises the value of true repentance. In the final service, the congregation asks that each individual should be judged favourably before his or her fate is finally sealed. The service ends with a sevenfold declaration, 'The Lord He is God, the Lord He is God' and a final, single note from the ram's horn.

A large proportion of the Jewish community still fast on the Day of Atonement and attend at least some of the synagogue services. At the end of the day there is a huge feeling of relief. The fast is over. Sin has separated the people from God, but through the fast, at-one-ment with God is attained. The Jewish people are reconciled with Him. After nightfall a huge meal is eaten and there is joy and laughter. At some stage it is usual to quote the verse from the Book of Ecclesiastes: 'Go your way, eat your bread with enjoyment and drink your wine with a merry heart; for God has already approved what you do' (Ecclesiastes 9:7).

Tasks

Writing tasks	Explain the reasons why fasting has replaced sacrifice. 'Fasting alone cannot restore a right relationship with God.' Assess this view.
Class discussion	Is the observance of Yom Kippur a psychologically healthy way of improving relationships between people, or does it just encourage negative feelings of guilt?

Glossary

Atonement	Reconciliation with God.
Kol Nidre	Prayer said in the Yom Kippur service which asks for release from rashly made vows.
Reconciliation	To make a relationship right, to set it on a proper footing. During Yom Kippur, Jews seek reconciliation both with each other and with God.
Rosh Hashanah	'Head of the year', Jewish New Year, which begins the period of reflecting on behaviour that culminates at Yom Kippur.
Selihot	Penitential prayers (prayers expressing remorse and seeking forgiveness).
Ten Days of Penitence	The period of ten days between Rosh Hashanah and Yom Kippur during which Jews reflect on their behaviour over the past year and seek forgiveness from one another.
Yom Kippur	Day of Atonement, a fast day during which Jews seek reconciliation with God and with each other.

Section 3

Aim of the section

This section will ask you to reflect on the role of Jewish life-cycle rituals in marking milestones and affirming Jewish commitment and identity, as well as some of the observances which make Jewish life distinctive.

You will need to consider:

1. **The role and importance of lifecycle rituals in maintaining Jewish identity, both as community celebration and as observance of commandments.**
2. **The practices associated with birth, coming of age, marriage and death.**
3. **The role of education in Jewish life.**
4. **The observance of laws relating to food, tephillin and mezuzah.**

Life Cycle Rituals

The importance of life-cycle rituals in maintaining Jewish identity

Throughout recorded history, people have moved through the landmasses of the world in pursuit of food, shelter and social advancement. Normally these immigrants have intermarried with the original inhabitants of the land and their customs have been lost within a few generations. In the British Isles, for example, there have been successive invasions by Celts, Romans, Angles, Saxons, Vikings and Normans. Over the centuries they have all intermingled and, as a result, their distinctive identities have disappeared.

The Jews have also moved from country to country and have a very ancient history. Yet, unlike most immigrants, they have managed to retain their original customs. There are nearly three hundred thousand people in the United Kingdom today who would identify themselves as Jews. Many others would say that they are 'half-Jewish' or that they have Jewish ancestry. We must ask how the Jews have remained a separate people when so many others have disappeared from history.

Both my grandfathers came from Russia. We had a small Jewish community in Ammanford and the shul (synagogue) services were held in a little room behind my grandfather's shop.'

Joyce, Swansea

'One of my grandfathers arrived here in the early years of the twentieth century. He was ten years old. He spent 9 months in school learning English and then he had a pack to take round with him to sell things. It's sad that we 'try to fit in'. Our grandparents couldn't. They were marked people with packs on their backs.'

Norma, Swansea

Why does Norma feel that it is sad that Jews try to fit in?

There is no simple answer, but one important element is the fact that Jews have conducted their everyday lives differently from their non-Jewish neighbours. We have already seen that they observe different festivals. They also have distinctive rituals to celebrate birth, coming of age, marriage and death. Because Jewish law covers every aspect of life, young people have always been strongly encouraged to seek marriage partners within the community. This has meant that the traditions are passed intact from generation to generation.

'When I was in school there were just two Jewish children in the class, myself and a boy. I thought it was good to be different as a child. Even now I still have a lot of friends who don't have any other friends who are Jewish, so they are very interested in finding out about my religion. Looking back I wish I'd been brought up in a bigger Jewish community. I mixed well with all my school friends and we are still close now. But I miss not having loads of Jewish friends now.'

Danielle, Swansea

'Everything happened on a Friday night and I wasn't allowed out on a Friday night. I used to concoct things so I could go out so I didn't feel out of it.'

Jewish teenager, Swansea

The problems and responsibilities of being different

This distinctiveness has not always been to the Jews' advantage. Human beings are uncomfortable with those who are different from them. Throughout history Jews have been regarded as peculiar and sinister. Evil rumours have been spread about them - for example it was said in the Middle Ages that the Jews poisoned the wells and were responsible for the Plague (which we now know was spread by rats). Even within living memory, in Nazi Germany the Jews were hunted down, herded into concentration camps and murdered. This hatred of Jews is known as Anti-Semitism. Jews are by no means the only people in the world who have been systematically persecuted, but anti-Jewish discrimination has been a frequent feature of Jewish experience for over two thousand years.

Steve emigrated to Israel from Wales.
'Of all the reasons I had for coming to live in Israel, Welsh anti-semitism was not one of them. I found the vast majority of the Welsh people I grew up with to be warm and friendly, and in retrospect, tolerant. I don't think it is a coincidence that every other chapel in Wales is called 'Zion'.'

The next two chapters, 'Family Life' and 'The Laws of Food and Daily Living', describe and explain some of the customs which have kept the Jews separate and apart from their neighbours. Two points must be emphasised at the outset:- Firstly, Jews do not follow these laws and customs in order to be different. This has been the result of keeping to the old ways, it is not the reason for doing so. They keep the commandments because they believe that that is what God has told them to do. It is as simple as that.

Secondly, it is mainly the laws and customs of the Orthodox which are described below. Many Jews nowadays are no longer observant. This does not mean that they cease to be Jews, since Jewish identity does not depend on belief, but they no longer follow the ways of their ancestors. There are also other groups, known as Reform or Liberal Jews, who practise their Judaism in a manner that interferes less with modern life. It must be understood that different Jews observe these rituals in different ways.

Family life

Aim

After studying this chapter you should be able to evaluate the role and importance in the Jewish family of the observance life-cycle rituals. You should be able to demonstrate clear knowledge and understanding of the customs and practices and to explore their key symbolism and key themes. You should be able to show the ways in which observance of them contributes to Jewish identity and family life. You should also be able to assess the role of education in the preservation of Jewish values and customs.

Many of the most important rituals of Judaism take place in the home. Jews have always emphasised the importance of family life. In the Creation story in the book of Genesis, woman was created as well as man because God said, 'It is not good that the man should be alone; I will make him a helper fit for him' (Genesis 2: 18). Among Orthodox Jews marriage and children are an essential part of the religious life and the major life-cycle events, birth, coming-of-age, marriage and death, take place in the context of the family.

Seminar topic

Explain some of the reasons why religions celebrate rites of passage.

Rituals of birth

The very first commandment to be found in the Bible is 'Be fruitful and multiply' (Genesis 1:28). The birth of children is a cause for rejoicing in a Jewish family. Every new baby is given a Hebrew name. This is generally related to their secular name, so Dafydd would be David and Louise Leah. In the synagogue and on formal religious documents, Jews are described by their Hebrew name and as son or daughter of their father. So Dafydd ap Sion would be David ben Johanan. Louise Evans, daughter of Jacob Evans, would be Leah bat Iacov. The new baby girl is given her name in the synagogue when her father is called up to read from the Torah scroll.

Circumcision

The baby boy is named at his circumcision. This ceremony, which involves the removal of the foreskin of the boy's penis, takes place at home when he is eight days old. According to Jewish law all male children must be circumcised. In the Book of Genesis, God commanded the patriarch Abraham that 'Every male among you must be circumcised...and it shall be the sign of the covenant between Me and you' (Genesis 17:10). The operation is performed by an expert (mohel) who has undergone considerable training.

However it is not being circumcised that makes the child a Jew. He is already Jewish by virtue of being born to a Jewish mother. Circumcision (Brit Milah) is merely a symbol that the baby has entered into the covenant.

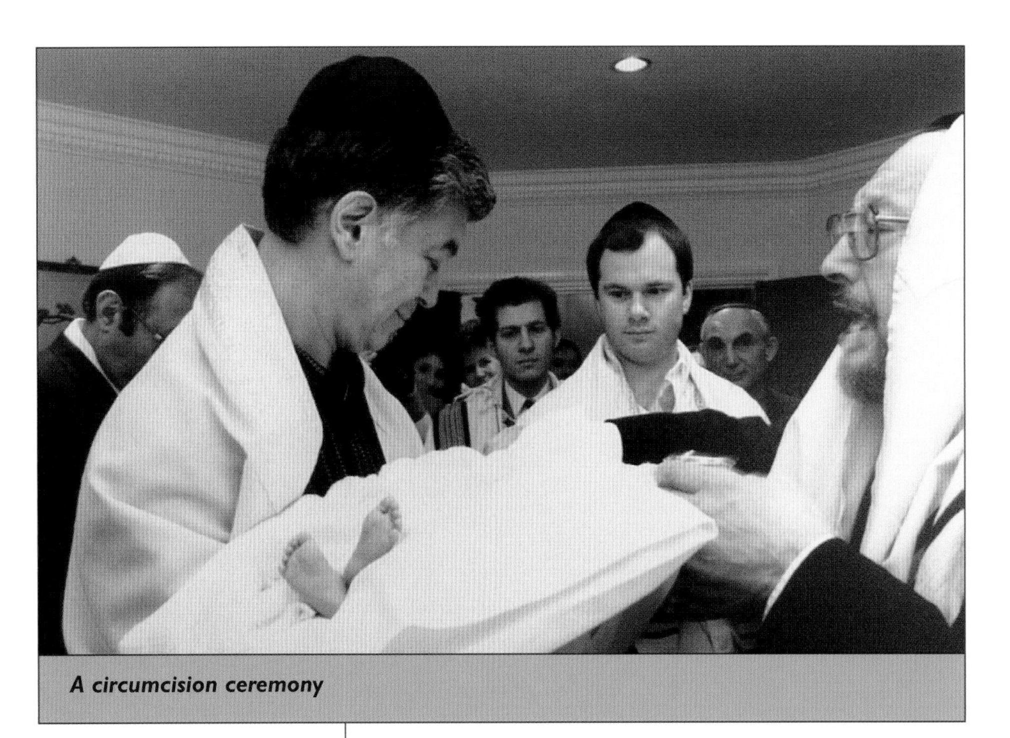

A circumcision ceremony

During the short accompanying service, the witnesses pray, 'That as this child has entered into the covenant, so may he enter into the Torah, the marriage canopy and into good deeds.' Afterwards there is a party. Often friends and relations will travel long distances to be present and there is much rejoicing that the Jewish tradition will continue through another generation.

Even the most non-religious Jews tend to have their sons circumcised. There is something very powerful about the mixture of pain, drawing blood, ancient symbolism and family celebration that is not easily abandoned.

Seminar topic

Explain some of the reasons why circumcision is such a powerful and meaningful ritual for Jewish families.

Redemption of the First-born

If the baby boy is the mother's first child, then another ritual is observed. This is known as the Redemption of the First-Born (Pidyon ha-Ben). According to the Book of Exodus, God said: 'Consecrate to me all the first-born; what ever is the first to open the womb among the people of Israel...is mine' (Exodus 13: 2). This is understood to mean that the baby belongs to God and must be bought back by his parents.

Redemption of the First-born

The ceremony takes place when the child is thirty-one days old. The baby is carried in and the father puts down a sum of money in front of the officiant or rabbi. He is asked whether he prefers to give up the baby or the money and he replies, 'I desire rather to redeem my son. Here you have the value of his redemption which I am bound to give you according to the Law.' The officiant is entitled to keep the money, but it is generally given to charity. Again the formal ceremony is followed by a party. This rite is observed only by the Orthodox, as Reform Jews feel that it no longer has any significance.

It will be noticed that both these rituals are performed for male children only. In recent years there have been some attempts to devise equally joyful celebrations for the birth of girl babies, but these are not part of the tradition and are not practised among the Orthodox.

Seminar topic

Which do you think is more important – ancient tradition or gender equality? Explain and justify your views.

Coming of age

Traditionally the education of boys has been different from the education of girls. It is a father's duty to educate all his children in the commandments, but girls' religious education has tended to emphasise the domestic side - how to keep a Jewish home. Boys, however, are expected to study the Bible, the Mishnah and the Talmud systematically, as well as their normal school subjects. Because Jewish law is extraordinarily complex, concentrated study is necessary. For centuries Jews have respected learning and huge sacrifices are made to encourage sons to be scholars.

This respect for education still exists today in all sections of the community. Among the non-Orthodox the emphasis has altered: they are anxious that their children do well at school and university and notoriously want them to prepare for the learned professions such as medicine and law. Meanwhile nothing has changed among the strictly Orthodox. They continue to stress the importance of traditional religious knowledge and an Orthodox boy can expect to study Mishnah and Talmud full-time until he is in his early twenties.

The Bar Mitzvah

At the age of thirteen a Jewish boy is considered to have attained adulthood. He is now obliged to keep the commandments for himself. He becomes a Son of the Commandment ('Bar Mitzvah'), and this coming of age is marked by being called up in the synagogue to recite the blessings over the Torah scroll and to chant some verses from the weekly reading. He may also read from the prophetic books and he will give a speech in which he will demonstrate his knowledge of the Mishnah and Talmuds.

For a child who has received an Orthodox education, this is not difficult. He will be able to read Hebrew as fluently as he can read his native language and he will be familiar with the passages. For non-Orthodox boys it is far more of a challenge. Hebrew in the Torah scrolls is written without vowels and a great many private lessons are necessary just to ensure that he can read the text. After the service there is generally a party. Friends and relations join the immediate family in celebration. The party can be a lavish affair, but there is no necessity for this. The important thing is that the young man is encouraged in his religious life and is seen to have taken his place within the community.

Jonathan carrying the Sefer Torah when he was Bar Mitzvah at the Western Wall in Jerusalem.

Joshua's Bar Mitzvah party in Cardiff.

Why do so many religions celebrate a child's symbolic entry into adulthood?

'For me it was like, instead of doing H.M.S. Pinafore for the drama club at camp, it was like doing a performance for God - much more serious but it's still a kind of a show. You memorise your lines, you memorise songs, you rehearse, and then there's just one performance, except the audience is your family and God, so it's a little more frightening and motivating!'

Jonathan, Swansea

Political situations in the world have sometimes affected the way the Bar Mitzvah is celebrated. A member of the Jewish community in Swansea explained that in a modern Bar Mitzvah it is not unusual to see a grandfather of 75 sharing a Bar Mitzvah with his grandson. The reason is that the grandfather may never have had a celebration because of the holocaust. Also, during the Cold War, Jewish children in Britain 'shared' a Bar Mitzvah in spirit with Jewish children in Russia who were not free to have the ceremony and couldn't leave the country.

When I had my Bar Mitzvah I felt a feeling of extra responsibility. I was looked on as a man from a religious point of view. Once you are Bar Mitzvah'd you take part a lot more in the religious ceremonies. You are taken into the community and viewed as an equal.

Although you have had your Bar Mitzvah and have become a man, education does not end there and there is still much to learn. Bar Mitzvah does not signify that you are now wise - it only means that you know right from wrong.

Joshua, Cardiff, Age 13

The Bat Chayil

Girls traditionally are regarded to have come of age when they reach their twelfth birthday, but there is no legal obligation to mark the occasion in any way. In some Orthodox communities a collective ceremony is held every year for all twelve-year old girls. This is known as a Bat Chayil ('Daughter of Life') service in which all the girls take their turn reading and saying a prayer. Among the non-Orthodox it is now the custom for daughters to become Bat Mitzvah ('Daughter of the Commandment') and the ceremony is often almost indistinguishable from that of their brothers. Again this trend is the result of the modern emphasis on women's' rights and it has no foundation in the tradition.

A girl celebrates her Bat Chayil.

What is the difference between Bat Chayil and Bar Mitzvah?

Jewish schools

Some Jews in the Diaspora elect to send their children to Jewish schools rather than to state schools. In Britain there have been Jewish Schools since the nineteenth century and around 15% of Jewish children in Britain currently attend a specifically Jewish School. Many of these schools have Voluntary Aided status, which means that the government provides part of their funding. Pupils at these schools study the ordinary national curriculum, but their religious education will be Jewish in nature, and there is lots of it. Such schools can organise themselves to be helpful to living a Jewish life. For instance, kosher food can be served in the canteen, mezuzot (mezuzahs) can be placed on doorposts, the school day can finish before sunset on Friday, even in winter, and Hebrew can be taught.

Many Jewish families feel that since Judaism touches all aspects of life, school should not be a place where religion is simply forgotten. Distinctively Jewish education is part and parcel of the Jewish way of life. The emphasis on it is one of the reasons that Judaism has survived down the centuries, even under persecution. Children who attend Jewish schools are constantly reminded of their identity and of the history of their people.

People who object to separate schools, including some Jews who do not send their children to Jewish schools, argue that educating pupils separately prevents the opportunity for different religions and cultures to learn from each other by mixing and developing friendships. Traditionally Jews have been wary of mixing in this way, needing to preserve their customs, and their ritual purity. However, Judaism has developed, and many non-Orthodox Jews feel there are great benefits, both to society and to Judaism, in mixing with non-Jews. They might also argue that it is the home rather than the school that should be the setting for learning about Jewish customs and beliefs.

To be honest, it is quite difficult for me to say what it means to be a Jewish teenager in the 21st century. For a start, I wonder whether I should think of myself as a "Jewish teenager"or a "teenage Jew."

In a pedantic sense, they are certainly very different. A "Jewish teenager" identifies first and foremost with the global unenfranchised; as I found out recently, teenage culture is the same, whether one is in London or Oslo. There are differences of course (for a start, every teenager there owns a tent and some heavy hiking equipment); but these tend to be regional variations, rather than due to any underlying distinction.

"Teenage Jew" suggests more of a path, a progression towards "mature Jew," a process of growth and development (apologies if this sounds like a biology lesson).

Increasingly, I think, the overarching teenage culture is displacing the Jewish one, not through a strong philosophical will to reject Judaism, but simply because it is easy, and it is at hand, and it simplifies what one should and shouldn't be concerned with. There is even a place in this teenage culture for religion; but in moderation.

I would say that, for me, Judaism is essentially a religious thing, more than a matter of social or cultural heritage. Of course, I appreciate the feeling of "brotherhood" — at school, I am one of the central members of the "North London Jew Crew," which, as it happens, includes an Arab — and it's nice to know that I can find a Shabbat meal in a foreign country, should I so choose.

But I think that these things exist only because there are Jews who still care about the religious aspect of Judaism. Not all Jews need be religious; but if none were, I think that Judaism, however you define it, would die a quick death.

Gabriel
Student, aged 16

An account by a 16-year old Jew of what it means to him to be Jewish.

Seminar topic

What are the main issues raised by Gabriel in his account of living a Jewish life in London? Why does he make a distinction between the ideas of a 'teenage Jew' and a 'Jewish teenager'?

Tasks

Writing tasks	Explain the Jewish attitude to Education.
	'Separate Jewish Schools are essential for the survival of Judaism in the Diaspora'. Evaluate this view.
Research task	Draw up a prospectus for a Jewish school in Wales, including a letter from the Head-teacher to parents explaining the ethos of the school. Consider issues such as the curriculum taught, the Jewish nature of all aspects of the school (e.g. collective worship, behavioural policy, food, religious education, spiritual and moral development) and the Welsh dimension to school life.

Marriage

Marriage is an essential part of Judaism. There are no Jewish monks or nuns. Everyone is expected to get married, to have a Jewish home and to rear Jewish children. In the past Jews almost invariably married other Jews. This was because Jews only mixed within their own communities and, as a result of anti-Semitism, Jews were not regarded as acceptable marriage partners. Today this has changed. The vast majority of Jews attend ordinary schools; they go to secular universities and they work side by side with non-Jews. As a result it has become increasingly common for Jews to 'marry out'. Today in America, for example, more than half the marriages that involve Jews are mixed marriages.

This has serious implications for the community. Jewishness is passed down from mother to daughter. Although it is possible to convert to Judaism, not every non-Jewish spouse is willing to do so. The result is that there is serious concern whether Judaism will survive in the future.

Tasks

Role play	Role-play a dialogue in which a Jewish woman tries to explain to her non-Jewish husband why his conversion to Judaism is important to her.
Research task	Using the Internet, discover the ways in which some Jews look for suitable marriage partners.

Judaism teaches that only a marriage between two Jews is valid as a Jewish marriage and most rabbis will officiate only if both partners are Jewish. The wedding can take place at home, in the synagogue or elsewhere, but it invariably includes five elements. Firstly, the marriage contract (Ketubah) has to be signed. This document dates from talmudic times and it settles a sum of money on the bride which the husband must pay in the event of a divorce.

Secondly, the bride and groom and both sets of parents stand under the bridal canopy (chuppah). This is a shelter, open on all four sides, symbolising the Jewish home that the couple will share together. Thirdly, wine is blessed and the young couple drink together from the same cup. Fourthly, the bridegroom puts a ring on the bride's finger and declares in front of all the witnesses 'Behold you are consecrated to me according to the laws of Moses and Israel'. Fifthly, the bridegroom stamps on a glass and breaks it. The meaning of this custom is obscure, but is thought to be a reminder of the destruction of the Jerusalem Temple in 70CE.

The marriage contract

Is a marriage contract a good idea? Explain your answer.

> 'When the Jewish bridegroom leaves the chuppah, it's not that he's got cold feet and decided to run away. It's because he's gone to bedeck the bride, to check that the woman under the veil is the one he wants to marry. This follows the story in the Torah.'
>
> Norma, Swansea

Hollywood has made many great films with Jewish themes. For example, 'Yentl' is about the difficulties faced by in the past by Jewish women in Eastern Europe and the victory of romantic love against all the odds.

Jewish weddings are very happy occasions. According to one of the traditional blessings which dates back to talmudic times, marriage is 'a state of joy and gladness, laughter and exultation, pleasure and delight, love, peace and friendship.' Although marriages are no longer arranged, among the Orthodox, parents and relatives will put considerable effort into introducing young people to likely marriage prospects. A Jewish wedding is the culmination of all these hopes and efforts.

> 'Everyone is happy at a wedding celebration. There's lots of singing and dancing. The bride sits on a chair and her friends lift her in the chair high into the air and carry her around the room. It's the same for the groom.'
>
> Norma, Swansea

The bride is lifted into the air during wedding celebrations.

Divorce

Jews also recognise, however, that marriages are not always happy and from biblical times divorce has been recognised. Procedures are laid down in the Book of Deuteronomy: 'When a man takes a wife and marries her, if she finds no favour in his eyes...he writes a bill of divorce (a Get) and sends her out of his house.' (Deut. 24:1). The woman is protected financially by her marriage contract and the purpose of the divorce document is to give proof that she is free to marry again. It is always the man who gives the document. According to Jewish law, a woman cannot initiate a divorce.

This did not matter so much in the past when Jews lived together in small villages. Then the community could put social and economic pressure on an unfaithful or abusive husband to ensure that he did give his wife her freedom. Today it is not so easy. If a man refuses his wife a divorce, there is little she can do about it. For this reason, non-Orthodox Jews regard the traditional laws of divorce as discriminatory against women and ignore them. Among the Orthodox, however, they are still observed, sometimes leaving women in very difficult situations.

Death

Judaism teaches that life is a gift from God. All forms of euthanasia are forbidden. However when all hope has gone and the patient is in great pain it is permissible to pray for death. The dying person is urged to make his or her final confession to God and ideally the final words will be the Shema: 'Hear O Israel, the Lord our God, the Lord is One'(see Chapter 5).

Traditionally the body is buried as soon as possible after death, preferably within twenty-four hours. In the intervening time it must never be left alone. It is covered with a sheet, a lighted candle is placed near the head and the close family make a symbolic tear in their clothes. Every community has a burial society, a group of volunteers who wash the body and prepare it for its final resting place. The corpse is dressed in a simple white shroud, because the tradition teaches that everyone is equal in death, and it is placed in a plain coffin.

The funeral service involves four elements: a short procession to the cemetery, the burial itself, a short eulogy and the recitation of the Kaddish prayer.

The Jewish graveyard, Prague.

Jews are always buried rather than cremated because of their belief in the Resurrection of the Dead at the end of time.

Mourner's Kaddish

And now, I pray thee, let the power of the Lord be Great, according as thou hast spoken. Remember, O Lord, thy tender mercies and lovingkindnesses; for they have been ever of old.

Mourner
Magnified and sanctified be His great name in the world which he hath created according to his will. May he establish his kingdom during your life and during your days, and during the life of all the house of Israel, even speedily and at a near time, and say ye, Amen.

Congregation and Mourner
Let his great name be blessed forever and to all eternity.

Mourner
Blessed, praised and glorified, exalted, extolled and honoured, magnified lauded be the name of the Holy One, blessed be he; though he be high above all the blessings and hymns, praises and consolations, which are uttered in the world; and say ye Amen.

Congregation
Let the name of the Lord be blessed from this time forth and for evermore.

Mourner
May there be abundant peace from Heaven, and life for us and for all Israel; and say ye, Amen.

Congregation
My help is from the Lord, who made Heaven and Earth.

Mourner
He who maketh peace in his high places, may he make peace for us and for all Israel; and say ye, Amen.

Braybrooke, M., *How to Understand Judaism*, SCM, 1995 p 36

During the procession Psalm 91 is recited. At the grave, all adult males present share the task of filling in the grave. The eulogy is a short address celebrating the merits of the dead person and the Kaddish is an ancient prayer of praise to God.

Task

Writing task	Re-write this prayer in your own words.

Once the funeral is over, the family spends seven days at home mourning and friends and neighbours come to the house to offer their condolences. This custom is known as 'Sitting shiva'. It is usual for the visitors to bring food with them so the family is not troubled with cooking during this sad time. Three times a day the mourners recite the Kaddish prayer. The next thirty days is a time of lesser mourning and life slowly returns to normal.

'When I was sitting shiva, all my family were gathered round me and stayed in my house for the week. Friends came round every evening for a service which was held in our house, and we all said the Kaddish prayer together. My friends brought food with them so I didn't have to worry about shopping or what we would all eat each day. It was very comforting to have my family with me all the time, and my friends to talk to about what had happened and what I was going through. I didn't have to go out and face the world and pretend to be OK. I could be myself and have the chance to mourn, and have support all around me when I most needed it.'

Jackie, Swansea

Every day for eleven months after the death of a parent the Kaddish prayer must be said. According to Jewish law, this prayer can only be recited when a quorum of ten men is present (i.e. a sufficient number of people to make the service viable — in Orthodox Judaism this means ten men). This is one reason why Orthodox synagogues have daily services. Mourners join the regular congregation and it is hoped that there will be at least ten men present every day. Finally the dead person is remembered every year on the Hebrew date of their death. A memorial candle is lit and Kaddish is again said. The non-Orthodox do not follow all these practices, but they will observe a period of mourning. In all sectors of the community it is still more usual for a Jewish person to choose burial over cremation and to want some sort of graveside service.

A headstone or memorial stone in the Jewish Cemetery, Swansea.

> 'You always wash your hands after you have been to the cemetery. You don't walk into your home without washing your hands first. However, the neighbours must think it odd when you are standing on the doorstep with a plastic bowl and a two handled cup in your hand!'
>
> Norma, Swansea

Task

Role play

Imagine you are an Orthodox Jew who has just lost a relation. Give an account to your class of your feelings and activities during the first nine days or so after the death.

Glossary

Bar/bat mitzvah 'Son/daughter of the commandment'. Rite of passage celebrated by Orthodox boys, and Reform Boys and girls, at 13 for boys and 12 for girls.

Bat Chayil 'Daughter of life'. In Orthodox Judaism a service in which all twelve year old girls take a turn at reading and saying a prayer.

Brit Milah Circumcision, the removal of the foreskin of eight-day-old boys as a sign of the covenant.

Get In Orthodox Judaism, a certificate of divorce issued by the husband.

Kaddish A prayer, said standing facing Jerusalem, which praises God. The Mourner's Kaddish is said for eleven months after the death of a parent of close relative, and on annivesaries of deaths.

Ketubah Marriage contract.

Pidyon ha-Ben 'Redemption of the first born', a ritual involving the father ritually choosing to give up some money rather than to give up his thirty-one day old son.

Rites of passage/ life cycle rituals Rituals that mark the passing from one state into another. Most religions have life-cycle rituals, marking birth, marriage and death. Some religions, like Judaism, have additional life-cycle rituals.

Sitting Shiva Staying at home for seven days after the death of a close relative, and receiving visitors on a low stool.

The laws of food and daily living

Aim

After studying this chapter you should be able to evaluate the role and importance in the Jewish family of the observance food laws (Kashrut), tephillin, mezuzah and dress codes. You should be able to demonstrate clear knowledge and understanding of Biblical roots of these practices and their varying interpretations in modern Judaism. You should also be able to show the ways in which observance of them contributes to Jewish identity and family life.

Everyone knows that Jews do not eat pork. In fact the laws of food and daily living are far more complicated than a single prohibition. They go back to a series of rules in the Hebrew Scriptures. These cover such topics as which animals are kosher ('permitted') and which trefah ('forbidden'), which categories of food may not be eaten together and what distinguishes a Jewish home. The rules have been discussed and refined over the centuries so that today the subject of kashrut (Jewish food laws), in particular, is highly complicated.

This has had an important effect on Jewish social life. In Shakespeare's 'Merchant of Venice', Shylock the Jew declares, 'I will buy with you, sell with you, talk with you, walk with you and so following. But I will not eat with you, drink with you or pray with you.' Even today Orthodox Jews follow the same pattern. Because the rules are complicated, they cannot eat in ordinary restaurants or in the houses of non-Jewish friends. For a social circle, Orthodox Jews must look within their own community.

However, it must be stressed that the majority of Jews today do not keep these laws in their entirety. Compromises are made. Sometimes a family will keep kosher (follow the law) at home, but will eat anything out. Sometimes they avoid pork and shellfish, but will eat anything else, and sometimes they ignore the rules altogether and their diet is indistinguishable from that of their non-Jewish neighbours. As in the previous chapter, it is Orthodox practice that will be described below.

> The story is told of a Jewish man who used to go to the YMCA in the mornings where he could have bacon secretly for breakfast. Before eating, he would always cut off a piece of bacon and put it in the ashtray. When asked why, he explained that his mother had told him "If you ever eat bacon, may the first mouthful choke you."

The food laws

According to the Creation story found in the Book of Genesis, originally human beings were given plants, seeds and fruits to eat (Genesis 1: 29). Only after the great flood did God give Noah and his family permission to eat meat (Genesis 9: 3-4). Even then, God declared 'Only you shall not eat flesh with its life, that is, its blood.' Vegetarianism, therefore, has always been an option for Jews and it is generally believed that in the last days of this Earth, when the Messiah (God's chosen king) arrives, human beings will return to a vegetable diet.

> 'The fruit that we associate with the Jewish people is the pomegranate. When you cut it, it has as many pips as the 613 rules. There is a multitude of seeds. It has turned out that the rules are good for health, hygiene and medicine. For example it's been discovered that the pomegranate is anti-carcinogenic and the juice has antiseptic qualities.'
>
> Norma, Swansea

In the meantime, the eating of meat is hedged about with restrictions. Firstly, in order to obey the prohibition against eating blood, the animal must be slaughtered in a way that encourages all the blood to flow out of the carcass. This involves slitting its throat cleanly with a very sharp knife and suspending it so the blood drains away. Kosher butchers are highly skilled and require considerable training. After the creature has been butchered, then the joints of meat must be salted to draw any remaining blood to the surface and then thoroughly rinsed. This treatment has the effect of drying out the meat, so Jewish cookery tends to emphasise stews and casseroles over roasts and grills.

Permitted and forbidden foods

Only certain animals may be eaten. The Book of Deuteronomy specifies that if an animal is to be used for food it must both chew the cud and have cloven feet (Deuteronomy 14: 6). This is why pork is forbidden. It is nothing to do with pigs harbouring tapeworm or pork going bad quickly in a hot climate. Although pigs have cloven hooves, they do not chew the cud and therefore they do not pass the Deuteronomic test. Similarly rabbit and hare are both forbidden (they neither chew the cud, nor do they have cloven feet), as is camel which does chew the cud, but has a flat pad rather than a split hoof. The animals that can be eaten, therefore, are cattle, sheep, goats and deer.

Scripture does not give a similar test for birds, but there are long lists of forbidden species. According to the Book of Leviticus these include the eagle, the osprey, the kite, the falcon according to its kind, every raven according to its kind, the ostrich, the nighthawk, the seagull...'(Leviticus 11: 13-14). It will be noticed that these are all birds of prey. There is no list of permitted birds, but birds which are usually eaten such as the chicken, turkey or duck are regarded as kosher. Fish is permitted provided it has both fins and scales. The Book of Deuteronomy declares 'Whatever does not have fins and scales you shall not eat; it is unclean for you' (Deuteronomy 14: 10). This means that Jews are forbidden all shellfish, such as shrimp, prawn, crab and lobster, as well as such creatures as eels and turtles.

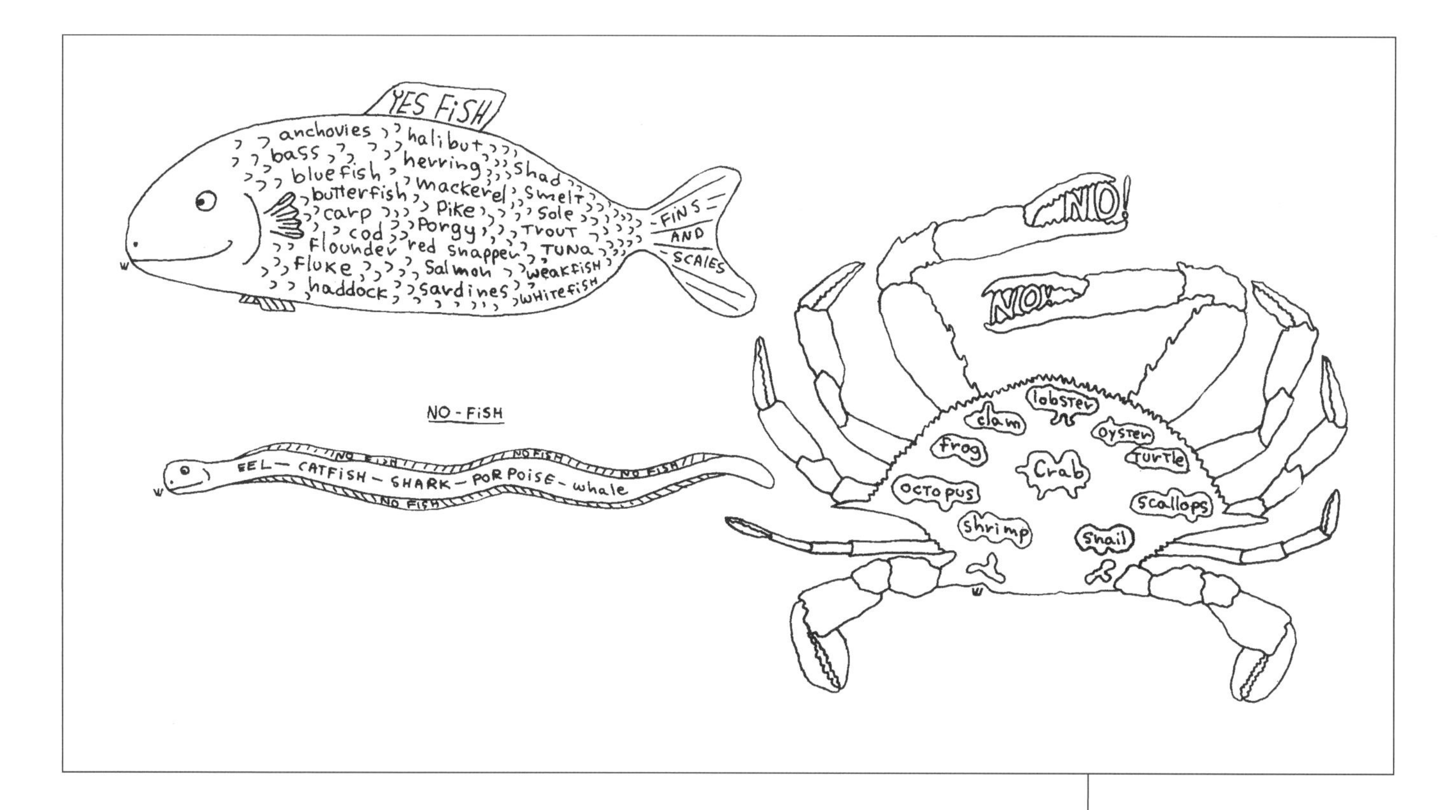

The verse 'You shall not boil a kid in its mother's milk' occurs three times in the Pentateuch, twice in the Book of Exodus (23:19 and 34: 26) and once in Deuteronomy (14: 21). Originally it may have been intended to prevent the Jews from following the pagan practice of slaughtering pregnant animals for their tender, unborn calves or of cooking newborn creatures in their mother's milk. In either case, it would have been regarded as a law enshrining the principle of kindness to animals. Over the years however, it has been understood to mean that meat food and milk food may not be eaten together at a single meal. Meat is understood to include poultry, but not fish.

The practical effect of this is that meat may not be served in any sort of cream sauce and a meat course cannot be followed by a milk pudding. So Orthodox Jews would never eat a cheese-burger, even if the burger had been made from kosher meat, because it violates the law of mixing. On the other hand, a creamy fish pie (as long as it was made with a fish that had both fins and scales) would be acceptable. Some foods, such as fish, are designated parve ('neutral') which means they can be mixed with either meat or milk products.

Buying kosher food

Most people do not know the exact ingredients of manufactured foods. For Orthodox Jews this is an important issue, since forbidden elements may have been included. For example, factory-made biscuits may be baked in tins that have been greased with pork fat. In order to reassure the Jewish housekeeper that an object is kosher, a system of certification has developed. Experts inspect factories and slaughterhouses to ensure that the laws are kept in every particular. Only when they are satisfied that a product contains nothing prohibited will they issue a certificate for it. A regular catalogue is published listing all acceptable manufactured foods, all shohet ('butchers') who sell shechitah ('correctly slaughtered') meat and all restaurants which serve kosher food.

Seminar topic

Role play a dialogue between a Jewish student and a non-Jewish student about Kashrut, which takes place after the Jewish student has been invited to a meal at her non-Jewish friend's house.

The kosher kitchen

A Jewish grandmother and her granddaughter make kreplach at Jewish New Year.

In the home, the kitchen must be organised so that there is no contact between meat foods and dairy foods. It is not enough to avoid serving them together in the same dish. Minute particles of food may remain on plates and cutlery after washing up and may then contaminate later meals. The solution is to have completely separate sets of crockery and cutlery for each type of food. Different working surfaces are used as well as different cooking utensils. Dirty plates must be washed up in different washing up bowls and stored in different cupboards. In the affluent society of today, a kosher kitchen may well have two washing up machines, two refrigerators and two freezers.

'Before I got married my mother took me shopping to buy all the bits and pieces I would need for my home. She asked me whether I would stick to the family tradition and have a red washing up bowl and red dishcloths for fleishig (meat dishes), and blue for milchig (milk dishes).
I thought there was no way I would keep all that. But once you've bought these things, you automatically use red for meat things and blue for milk . . . wouldn't dream of not doing this. And so the culture continues.'

Jacqui, Swansea

If mistakes are made and one set of utensils is contaminated by the other, the law prescribes how the situation can be put right. After cleaning the contaminated object thoroughly, all traces of the offending food can be removed either by burning it off with a blow-torch or by immersing it for several minutes in a large pan of boiling water. Neither alternative is possible for china or glass, which would break under the necessary high temperature. The householder has no alternative but to give the plate away to a charity shop or to non-Jewish friends.

The situation is complicated still further by the laws of Pesach (see Chapter 6). During the seven or eight days of the festival, it is forbidden to eat any chametz ('yeast / raising agent') and none should be kept in the house. It is therefore the custom to conduct a thorough spring clean throughout the house, removing all crumbs. The usual crockery and cutlery is put away and special, yeast-free sets are brought out for the duration of the season. Again there have to be two different sets. It is an enormous amount of work for the housewife, particularly as the festival is celebrated with a large elaborate ritual meal on the first and (outside the Land of Israel) the second night.

Strictly Orthodox Jews keep all these laws as a matter of course, but it is a serious financial commitment. Quite apart from the extra equipment involved, shohet have to be trained and the whole inspection process involves a considerable bureaucracy. Consequently kosher food is substantially more expensive than food bought in a regular supermarket.

Kosher cuisine

There is no particular kosher cuisine. Different Jewish communities throughout the world eat different dishes that tend to be influenced by the eating patterns of the nations in which they live. In the United States and Britain, salt beef, dill cucumbers, potato pancakes, beetroot soup and fish dumplings are all considered to be 'Jewish food'. In fact, they are merely the dishes of Eastern Europe, where the majority of Anglo-American Jewish families originate. In contrast Oriental Jews tend to eat falafel, rice and couscous. Any national cuisine has the potential to be kosher and New York, in particular, has a huge array of kosher restaurants, including Chinese, Mexican and French.

In the Middle Ages one of the reasons Jews were accused of witchcraft was because they seemed to enjoy better health than the rest of the population. It is probable that this annual purge was in a large measure responsible. But again it must be emphasised that the laws of Kashrut have nothing to do with health. The reason Jews follow them is because they believe God has commanded them to do so.

Jewish law and daily living

Jewish law covers every aspect of life. The Book of Deuteronomy declares that God's words, his law, should be bound 'as a sign upon your hand and they shall be as an emblem on your forehead. And you shall write them on the doorposts of your house and on your gates' (Deuteronomy 6: 8-9). This verse is used as part of the Shema (the prayer that begins 'Hear O Israel') and it is recited at least twice every day. The pious Jew will say it first thing in the morning when he rises and the last thing at night when he goes to bed. Ideally it is also said as his last words on his deathbed.

The prayer is not understood just as a metaphor: it does not just mean that Jews should be constantly aware of God's commandments. Rather, the words are taken literally and are followed in the laws of tephillin and mezuzah.

Tephillin and mezuzahs

Tephillin are small boxes containing biblical verses written on parchment by hand. The verses are Exodus 13: 1-16, Deuteronomy 6: 4-9 and Deuteronomy 11: 13-21. These boxes are attached to leather straps. One is put over the head so the box lies between the eyes and the other is wound in a special way around the left arm so that the box faces the heart. Every weekday morning Orthodox men perform this ritual while they recite the prescribed prayers.

The Mezuzah is not really the container, but the scroll inside the container with the Shema inscribed upon it.

Another small box containing a parchment is known as a mezuzah. The verses here are Deuteronomy 6: 4-9 and 11: 13-21 (the same passages that make up the Shema prayer). On the back of the parchment is written the word Shaddai ('Almighty'). The box is nailed on the right-hand doorpost and, in an Orthodox home, there is one for every room in the house except for the bathroom. It is placed two-thirds of the way up the doorpost, at a slanting angle, pointing into the room. Thus every time a Jewish person moves around the house, he or she is reminded of God's law. Again, this is a very ancient custom. A mezuzah was found by archaeologists at the site where the Dead Sea Scrolls were discovered.

Although only the Orthodox place a mezuzah on every door, almost everyone who has any affiliation with the Jewish community nails one on their front door. In areas where there is a large Jewish population, such as Golders Green in London, or in certain areas of Manhattan, New York, a mezuzah can be seen on a significant proportion of the flats and houses.

Clothing and appearance

Orthodox men also wear distinctive clothing. The skull cap (Kippah or Yarmulkah) only goes back to the twelfth century CE, but is one of the most instantly recognisable signs that a man is Jewish. There are also laws concerning facial hair. According to the Book of Leviticus (19:27), it is forbidden to cut the corners of the beard. It is understood among the strictly Orthodox that the side curls should be allowed to grow and these are frequently seen on young boys. Adults tend to twist them round and tuck them behind their ears so they are not visible.

In the Book of Numbers (15:37-38), Jews are instructed to make fringes on the corners of their garments and consequently Orthodox men wear an undergarment which has tzitzit ('fringes') on all four corners. A special blessing is said when it is put on each day. In addition tzitzit are placed on each corner of the tallit ('shawl') which Jewish men wear when they pray. These fringes remind Jews of the 613 mitzvot.

Women are not commanded to wear any specific clothes, although the Orthodox dress modestly. Skirts cover the knee and sleeves the elbow. Married women cover their hair completely and, rather than use a scarf, they often wear a very glamorous wig. Nonetheless Jewish women are not so recognisable in their clothing as Jewish men.

In the past, most recently in Nazi Germany, Jews were compelled to wear a distinctive badge, but today the vast majority of Jews are indistinguishable from their neighbours. Those who do wear beards, fringes or skullcaps do so solely because they believe that in so doing they are following the commandments of God for the Jewish people.

Tasks

Writing tasks	
	Explain how the distinctive dress code has helped to maintain Jewish identity
	Assess the validity of the view that Jewishness is better expressed through moral behaviour than through the rituals of daily living.

Jewish children in the northern Israeli town of Safed.

Children are special in Judaism. Without children, the religion could not be passed to the next generation.

Glossary

Dead Sea scrolls	Important first century Jewish documents found near the archaeological site of Qumran, next to the Dead Sea. The documents provide much information about how some Jews lived during the Second Temple Period.
Kashrut	The Jewish food laws.
Kosher	'Permitted', food that can be eaten according to the rules in the scriptures.
Mezuzah	Parchment, with the Shema inscribed on it, in a container attached to doorposts and gates.
Tephillin	Parchment inscribed with the Shema and contained in leather boxes bound onto the forehead and left arm of Orthodox Jewish males.

Material for the Synoptic Unit (A2)

Throughout your study of Judaism your teacher will have been alerting you to the information which you should bear in mind for the Synoptic Module which will be assessed at the end of your study of A2.

The assessment for the Synoptic module requires you to write an essay under controlled conditions on a specified aspect of either Religious Authority, or Religious Experience, or Life, Death and Life after Death. This essay should draw on at least two areas of study, because you are required to be able to sustain a critical line of argument, which may involve comparing and contrasting different areas of study.

As well as having the required knowledge and understanding of one of the three areas identified for synoptic assessment, you will need to demonstrate some critical reflection and the ability to sustain a line of argument.

Religious Authority

The idea of Religious Authority runs through the topics in this book. God is the ultimate authority for Jews, and from an Orthodox point of view, God's will is made clear in the Torah. The Mishnah and Talmuds also have authority as divinely inspired scriptures that are used to help in understanding the revelation of the Torah. For non-Orthodox Jews, human reason and modern thought have authority too, and can also be used to try to understand the revelation. Jewish belief in the authority of the revelation can be seen in the way they practice their religion, and the extent to which they keep the 613 mitzvot shows where they believe authority is ultimately located. The authority of the synagogue and of the home should also be evaluated, as should the role of the rabbi in ritual life.

Religious experience

This book shows that Judaism is a religion that is based on religious experience. The experience of God that certain key individuals such as Abraham, Moses and the Prophets had, forms the foundation of Jewish belief and practice. For ordinary Jews today religious experience comes through prayer, pilgrimage, the observance of the festivals and the keeping of the mitzvot. Distinctive to Jewish religious experience is the notion of God acting in history. Thus in the Hebrew Bible, events which occur are experienced as God's retribution or reward. Sometimes post-biblical events, for example the Creation of the State of Israel in 1948, are seen in this light too.

Ideas of life, death and life after death

The focus in Judaism is on life, rather than on death. The mourning prayer of Kaddish does not mention the dead, but focuses on the greatness of God, even at a time of suffering for the mourner. The funeral itself allows for intense grief, and the dead are remembered annually. Belief in a life after death has not been central to Judaism, though from the Second Temple Period onwards the afterlife is seen as something to look forward to. Many Jews believe in the resurrection of the body at the end of time, and so burial is more common than cremation. For many, the idea of life after oneself through one's children, who are the children of Israel, is as important or perhaps more important than any idea of personal survival.

Bibliography

Alexander, P.S., (1984) *Textual Sources for the Study of Judaism*, Manchester, Manchester University Press

Close, Brian, (1991) *Judaism: A Student's Approach to World Religions*, London, Hodder and Stoughton

Cohn-Sherbok, L. & D., (1994) *Judaism: A Short History*, Oxford, Oneworld

Cohn-Sherbok, L. & D., (1999) *Judaism: A Short Introduction*, Oxford, Oneworld

Cohn-Sherbok, L. & D., (1999) *A Short Reader in Judaism*, Oxford, Oneworld

Cohn-Sherbok, D., (1999) *Judaism*, London, Routledge

De Lange, N., (1984) *Atlas Of the Jewish World*, London, Phaidon

Epstein, Isidore, (1990) *Judaism*, Harmondsworth, Penguin

Pilkington, C., (2003) *Judaism*, Teach Yourself Books, London, Hodder Headline PLC

Solomon, Norman, (1996) *Judaism: A Very Short Introduction*, Oxford, Oxford University Press